Excellence through Mind-Brain Development

Expansion of happiness is the purpose of life.
— Maharishi Mahesh Yogi ([1963] 2001, p. 48),
world-leading expert on higher human development

The timeless message of this research-based book is that we are all born with a huge potential for development, and that unlocking this potential provides any woman or man with the foundation for stable happiness and high performance in any profession or activity.

Excellence through Mind-Brain Development

The Secrets of World-Class Performers

HARALD S. HARUNG, PhD.

and

FREDERICK TRAVIS, PhD.

GOWER

Gower Applied Business Research
Our programme provides leaders, practitioners, scholars and researchers with thought provoking, cutting edge books that combine conceptual insights, interdisciplinary rigour and practical relevance in key areas of business and management.

Published by
Gower Publishing Limited
Wey Court East
Union Road
Farnham
Surrey, GU9 7PT
England

Gower Publishing Company
110 Cherry Street
Suite 3-1
Burlington, VT 05401-3818
USA

www.gowerpublishing.com

British Library Cataloguing in Publication Data
A catalogue record for this book is available from the British Library

Library of Congress Cataloging-in-Publication Data
Harung, Harald S.
Excellence through mind-brain development: the secrets of world-class performers / by Harald S. Harung and Frederick Travis.
pages cm
Includes bibliographical references and index.
ISBN 978-1-4724-6201-5 (hardback) -- ISBN 978-1-4724-6202-2 (ebook) -- ISBN 978-1-4724-6203-9 (epub) 1. Performance--Psychological aspects. 2. Neuropsychology. 3. Success. I. Travis, Frederick. II. Title.
BF481.H376 2015
158--dc23

2015003791

ISBN: 9781472462015 (hbk)
ISBN: 9781472462022 (ebk – PDF)
ISBN: 9781472462039 (ebk – ePUB)

MIX
Paper from responsible sources
FSC® C013985

Printed in the United Kingdom by Henry Ling Limited, at the Dorset Press, Dorchester, DT1 1HD

Reviews for *Excellence through Mind-Brain Development*

In this interesting book Harung and Travis have managed to convey their message in a readable way so that a layman can understand it. Personally, I liked the simple and concrete results they present from their research on world-class performers and higher mind-brain development.

Ingrid Kristiansen, Norway, only track runner who held world records for 5000m, 10000m, half-marathon, and marathon at the same time

Harung and Travis introduce a compelling aspect of world-class performance in leaders – higher mind-brain development. They do so in a manner that busy senior executives can understand and apply. This book is essential reading for leaders wishing to ensure comprehensive and sustainable world-class excellence in themselves and their organizations.

Lynne Sedgmore CBE, Chief Executive of 157 Group of UK colleges and former CEO of the UK Center for Excellence in Leadership

In this book, Harung and Travis offer a lucid, research-based, very readable, and convincing advocacy for mind-brain development as a discriminator between ordinary and world-class performance in several fields from athletics to management. This is a book for laypersons as well as professionals. I particularly liked the simple and concise definitions of terms and ideas and the vivid examples to illustrate the abstract concepts.

Susanne R. Cook-Greuter, acknowledged researcher in higher self-development, USA

The inner realm of man is highly structured and open to scientific exploration. In the investigations of this book, peak experiences are recognized as essential for peak performance. Transcendental Meditation, practiced by the author of this endorsement for 55 years, is a scientific technique to systematically produce peak experiences. Practiced regularly, this technique can make peaks become ordinary. The result is a state of consciousness in which effortless high performance and joy is a daily experience even during the most mundane and trivial chores of day-to-day living.

Prince Blücher von Wahlstatt, Germany

I find the research findings regarding top-level performers among athletes, musicians, and executives very interesting. As a former CEO the findings among managers are of particular relevance to me. I did personally participate in the research, going through a number of the professional tests myself, with which results I could most certainly identify.

Tor Dahl, former CEO of international staffing company Manpower in Norway, the Nordic countries, and Europe

This book reveals the ultimate secret to success in every field—integrated brain functioning. If you want to know how to be the very best you can be, then read this book.

David Lynch, filmmaker, USA

Peak performance researchers, such as Dr. Harald Harung and Dr. Frederick Travis, have uncovered the key active ingredient in peak performance—mind-brain development. They found an integrated state of brain functioning to be a common neurophysiological signature in the world-class athletes, CEOs, and musicians they have studied.

David K. Williams, *Forbes Magazine*, USA

Take heart, conscious people everywhere. Harung and Travis have written the book you have been waiting for! Through their exhaustive scientific and academic research, they establish the undeniable link between higher mind-brain development and superior performance in business, sports, and music. This is a major breakthrough—that is just plain fascinating.

Patricia Aburdene, USA, one of the world's leading social forecasters

Contents

List of Figures

List of Tables

Acknowledgments

We would like to thank all those who have made valuable contributions to this book: Craig Berg, Warren Blank, Kevin Bækkevold, Ken Chawkin, Susanne Cook-Greuter, Ken Daley, David Goodman, Meredith Greiner, Laurence Habib, Park Hensley, Svein Jacobsen, Dag Kaas, John Kremer, Stefan Lagrosen, Yvonne Lagrosen, Magne Lerø, Joar Opheim, Anne Marte Pensgaard, Jane Schmidt-Wilk, Knut L. Seip, Kevin Selmes, Neil Sims, Per Ø. Staff, Ken Walton, and Bill Witherspoon. In particular, we would like to thank Morten Hvidsten for coordinating the research and translating responses from Norwegian to English, Ragnhild Boes for doing the field testing and participating in the analysis of the data for the study on athletes, and Sue Brown, Gerry Geer, Sebastian Harung, Dennis Heaton, Jim Karpen, and Craig Pearson for their many suggestions for improvements of the manuscript.

Financial support has been provided by Maharishi University of Management, Oslo and Akershus University College of Applied Sciences, G. C. Rieber Funds, and Swedish Foundation for International Cooperation in Research and Higher Education.

Origin of Research Instruments and New Theories

Drs. Bob Cranson, Charles N. Alexander, Harald S. Harung, Ken Chandler, and Dennis Heaton conceived and developed the *Survey of Peak Experiences*; Dr. Frederick Travis the *Brain Integration Scale*; Dr. Harald S. Harung the *Unified Theory of Performance*, the *Unified Theory of Leadership*, and the *Unified Theory of Collective Performance*; and Dr. Harald S. Harung and Dr. Frederick Travis the *Performeasure* assessment.

Trademarks

Corporation, a 501(c)(3) non-profit educational organization. Performeasure® is the trademark of Brain Integration Systems, LLC, Fairfield, Iowa, USA.

About the Authors

Dr Harald S. Harung

Dr Harald S. Harung teaches management, ethics, and peak performance to classes of up to 500 students at Oslo and Akershus University College of Applied Sciences (17,000 students) in Norway. He has for more than 30 years been working as a researcher and consultant within human performance development, both on an individual and organizational level. Dr Harung has lectured worldwide and his research on world-class performers has received support from both public institutions and private companies. Participants and collaborators in his seminars include such companies as Manpower, PricewaterhouseCoopers, Amoco, Den Norske Bank, Ericsson, Norsk Hydro, Santa Maria, Telenor, Toyota, and Xerox. He has worked with or lectured to organizations such as Academy of Management, European Institute for Advanced Studies in Management, Finnish Marketing Association, Indian Institute of Management, Mongolia University of Science and Technology, Norwegian School for Sport Sciences (*Norges Idrettshøgskole*), Norwegian National Olympic Training Center (*Olympiatoppen*), University of Wales at Aberystwyth, and World Productivity Congress (Sweden, Scotland, and Turkey).

Dr Harung holds a PhD. from University of Manchester. He has worked as a researcher at Oxford University, naval officer, CEO of an engineering firm, and founder and president of an international business college, and has been one of the editors of *The Learning Organization – An International Journal*. Dr Harung has published papers in such journals as *Journal of Managerial Psychology*, *Cognitive Processing*, *Consciousness and Cognition*, *Management Decision*, *Scandinavian Journal of Medicine and Science in Sports*, and *The Learning Organization: An International Journal*. His book *Invincible Leadership* has been published in USA (MUM Press) and in the Czech Republic (Euromedia).

Dr Frederick Travis

Dr Frederick Travis earned his Masters and PhD. in Psychology from Maharishi University of Management, Fairfield, Iowa, USA. He had a two-year post-doctoral position at University of California, Davis and the VA Medical Center in Martinez, CA with Dr Irwin Feinberg exploring brain functioning. At the conclusion of his post-doctoral position, he returned to Maharishi University of Management to teach and direct research at the Center for Brain, Consciousness, and Cognition.

Dr Travis has authored over 70 papers and numerous conference presentations that investigate the relation between natural human development and lifestyle choices on brain functioning. Journals include *Biological Psychology, Consciousness and Cognition, Cognitive Processing, Dreaming, Sleeping, International Journal of Neuroscience, International Journal of Psychophysiology, Journal of Trauma and Stress, Scandinavian Journal of Medicine and Science in Sports, Neuroquantology, Journal of Clinical Psychology*, and *American Journal of Hypertension*. He has lectured at the New York Academy of Science and at universities and conferences in a large number of countries: Almost every state in the USA and Canada; Columbia and Brazil in South America; the United Arab Emirates, Turkey, and Cyprus in the Middle East; Mongolia and China in the East; Italy, Spain, Germany, England, the Netherlands, Switzerland, Sweden, and Norway in Europe.

Dr Harald S. Harung: www.harvest.no
Dr Frederick Travis: www.drfredtravis.com

Prologue

Everyone wants excellence and happiness. We all admire world-class performers like Sir Paul McCartney (music), David Lynch (film), Oprah Winfrey (entertainment), Pelé (soccer), Sir Roger Bannister (running), Billie Jean King (tennis), Sir Alex Ferguson (management), Stephen Covey (management consulting), Magnus Carlsen (chess), and Marit Bjørgen (cross-country skiing). Yet, today world-class performance is rare.

By looking deeply at successful athletes, managers, and musicians, we found the secret of world-class performance: Excellence in any profession or activity primarily depends on the *single* factor of high mind-brain development. Factors like education, practice, and incentives simply cannot explain world-class performance, research shows.

By mind-brain development we mean a much more comprehensive transformation than what is commonly understood—we are talking about a sequence of fundamental shifts to new realities in the way our brain functions and in the way we look upon ourselves, others, and the world. For success, who we *are* is much more important than the knowledge, skills, and relationships we *have* and what we *do*. With higher mind-brain development, our knowledge and skills become more useful, our relationships more enriching, and our actions more effective.

This book combines mind-brain research with inspiring descriptions of peak experiences that underlie top performance. You will read that top performers have a much more orderly, restfully alert, and economic brain than average performers. This book will show you the many benefits of higher mind-brain development and how to attain such development in an enjoyable and effortless way.

Preface

Messi jumps high into the air and heads the ball elegantly into the goal. LeBron James, while falling backwards, sends the ball in a perfect arc into the basket. Walt Disney provides moments of happiness to millions of people around the world. Benny Goodman makes the clarinet famous in the big band era. Ole Einar Bjørndalen delivers another astounding performance in biathlon skiing and shooting, winning his 53rd medal in Olympic Games or world championships. The first automobile, Mercedes-Benz, is made using the slogan "The best or nothing." Antonio Vivaldi's violin concert *The Four Seasons* is a true masterpiece that uplifts the listeners everywhere. Mahatma Gandhi leads the peaceful process of making India independent.

It is thrilling to see excellence! And we all aspire to high levels of performance in our own job or hobby. Such aspirations are completely human and natural. However, we may feel that top-level performance is only for a few select individuals who are "born" with genius. The good news is that, based on extensive scientific research, high performance seems to be generally available—generally available because this book identifies *one* factor that is the basis of high levels of achievement in *all* professions and areas of life. This single factor is *mind-brain development*. The brain and mind are our link with the world—experiences and behavior are governed by our level of brain and mental refinement. Higher mind-brain development *spontaneously* expresses itself in higher performance. Fortunately, it is simple to facilitate mind-brain development in practice.

The reality revealed by research is that other factors—commonly thought to underlie top performance—cannot explain greatness. Factors like level of education, extent of practice, or the size of incentives. Research shows that education accounts for only 1 percent of performance levels, work experience only 3 percent, and age in adults 0 percent.

The discovery of one "active ingredient" in world-class performance has emerged over our 10 year collaboration—Harald bringing in management models and thinking, and Frederick bringing in research on brain maturation and the association of brain functioning with behavior. Together we have recorded brain waves and interviewed professional musicians in Swedish and Norwegian concert halls, measured professional athletes who for three seasons had placed amongst the ten best in the world (most of them with gold medals in Olympic Games or world championships), and sat in the CEO's office of major corporations explaining how brain integration is the basis of creative solutions and continued progress in the challenging business world.

Find a comfortable chair and begin an exploration of how *you* can take control of your success, and begin to aim high in life. You can easily learn to develop the basic factor that has been found in world-class performers. We wish you happy reading and hope that this book will be useful for fundamentally improving your performance.

Dr Harald S. Harung and Dr Frederick Travis
Fairfield, Iowa, USA, 9 April, 2015

This Book at a Glance

1. Everyone wants excellence and happiness.
2. The typical human being has an extensive developmental potential. This potential exists because we have not unfolded our deepest mental levels.
3. The Unified Theory of Performance, presented in this book, states that higher mind-brain development forms the basis of higher performance in *all* professions and fields of human activity.
4. This theory has four dimensions: Level of brain functioning, individual psychology, frequency of peak experiences, and the development of the social context of performance (the organizations and society in which we operate). Peak experiences are the most happy and fulfilling moments in life.
5. The four dimensions act synergistically and support higher performance and higher quality of life as we turn our attention to our chosen areas of life.
6. Brain functioning lies at the basis of the two mental dimensions —better psychology and peak experiences.
7. The factors normally thought to underlie high performance—education, age, practice and work experience, and incentives—have little or no effect on mind-brain development and therefore on the level of performance.
8. Today, mind-brain development is found to *freeze* in the early twenties, because society normally does not provide the necessary experiences that foster growth beyond the genetically programmed development between birth and the age of 25.
9. A better psychology forms the basis of temporary peak performance in narrow domains, e.g., in management or a science. In contrast, lasting peak experiences provide the potential for sustained world-class performance in a wide range of human activities.
10. There are many techniques for exploring inner psychology. They have different procedures and results in different brain wave patterns, and so have different benefits for practical life. In general, the more focused a mental method is, the more restricted will be its effect.
11. The Transcendental Meditation technique provides a systematic and effortless procedure for enlivening Transcendental Consciousness —the most fundamental and expanded mental level. Transcending simultaneously develops *all* four dimensions underlying performance, as well as the performance itself, as shown by research.
12. By developing higher mind-brain maturation in a sufficient number of individuals it should be possible to eliminate many of the problems plaguing today's society and instead create widespread excellence and happiness.

Chapter 1

Introduction: A Vision of Possibilities through Higher Human Development

I have no doubt whatever that most people live, whether physically, intellectually or morally, in a very restricted circle of their potential being. They make use of a very small portion of their possible consciousness. Much like a man who, out of his whole organism, should get into the habit of using and moving only his little finger.

— *William James, father of American psychiatry (1963, pp. 275–276)*

Peak Experiences and World-class Performance

The 30 km freestyle cross-country skiing race at the Winter Olympics at Lillehammer was held on 14 February 1994. Many thoughts ran through the head of the runner Thomas Alsgaard when he woke up. Would he have a good race? Would he win his first Olympic gold medal? He had been preparing for this event since childhood with innumerable hours of physical and technical training, and his father as his first coach. As early as at the age of three Thomas entered a race for five year olds, and beat them all!

Thomas had also spent many hours mentally visualizing how he would master the many aspects and phases of the 30 km race. Cross-country skiing is a sophisticated sport where the most effective way of moving the body depends on many factors, several of which are continually changing throughout a race: Slope of uphill; snow, rain or wind; condition of the snow (e.g., new or old, fine-grained or coarse, firm or loose); and the temperature of the snow and air. Despite all these physical and mental preparations, was he really ready? Would he be able to run faster than Bjørn Dæhlie? Bjørn was his major competitor who for several years had been dominating male cross-country skiing in the world.

When Alsgaard woke up in Lillehammer that morning, he felt as if something was wrong. He had a strange feeling, one he had never had before.

The conditions were ideal for cross-country skiing—the temperature was below freezing and the sun was shining. Runners from many countries lined up and started one by one at a fixed time interval. Once Alsgaard started the race, it quickly became clear that he was performing at an unprecedented level. He felt intensely happy. He was racing effortlessly. And yet there he was, out ahead of everyone, including Dæhlie.

The feeling of elation and ease had, in fact, begun when he woke up in the morning. As it turned out, there was nothing "wrong" with it—he simply had no way to understand it or know how it would affect his performance. Even the television reporter remarked how effortlessly Alsgaard seemed to be moving along, as if in a dance. Alsgaard won the race easily, with the exceptional time of 1:12:26.4. Dæhlie was a distant second, 47.2 seconds behind.

This race marked Alsgaard's international breakthrough. He went on to win a total of 11 gold medals in Olympic Games or world championships, making him one of the world's most successful skiers ever. He is widely regarded as the master of free technique cross-country skiing, a technique that resembles ice skating.

Alsgaard was enjoying what psychologists call a *peak experience* and what athletes call the experience of the *zone*. Peak experiences typically involve intense inner happiness (bliss) along with effortless—and superior—outer performance. The American psychologist Abraham Maslow, the first to study this category of experiences systematically, identified a number of other qualities of these joyous moments: Feelings of wonder and awe, wholeness and integration, even transcendence of time and space. During such moments, one feels that life is endowed with special meaning (Maslow, 1968).

This was Alsgaard's first major peak experience—and he was astonished by how easy and joyful his performance was. Thomas became known as the *joy runner*, since he performed best when he felt racing was fun. "It is a game," he says. "Sport is play. The day it becomes serious, then you are done. This is what differentiates the very best from the next best" (Harung, 2012, p. 48). And sometimes when racing was not so much fun, he would use that competition to analyze, to try to discover what was wrong, so that he could adjust and make sure he did better in the next competition. Related to Alsgaard's peak experiences was his sense of being guided by his intuition:

> *Often it is just acting on gut feeling and instinct. ... I have made very many choices without really knowing why, but I had a good feeling, and*

> *then in hindsight it becomes clear that it was just this little deviation, just this change that was needed to perform at top.*

Alsgaard credited much of his success to good luck. He won more than half of his gold medals in Olympic Games or world championships with a margin of less than one second. Alsgaard regards luck as an attribute, since the same people seem to have good fortune all the time.

Alsgaard has reported many peak experiences (Alsgaard, 2008). "When everything is at the very highest level, then I feel invincible," he says. "The up-hills are not long enough nor steep enough. [It's an] extremely good sensation." He has also experienced greatly expanded awareness, deep relaxation along with dynamic activity, spontaneous right action, and a sense of perfection. Here is the 30-km race in his own words:

> *The senses are so open that you have the ability to receive signals that are almost scary: In a way, it is a "high." I receive an unbelievable amount of information. Much, much more—10–20 times more information—than what I manage if I sit down and concentrate and try to perceive things. But I am so relaxed. And the more relaxed I am, the more information I register.*

Other Examples of Peak Experience and Peak Performance

We find examples of peak experiences giving rise to peak performance in all sports. One of the classic examples occurred in 1954, in one of history's greatest sports breakthroughs. On May 6, in Oxford, England, Sir Roger Bannister became the first person in the world to run a mile in under four minutes. He describes his exhilaration and effortlessness in these words (Bannister, 2004, pp. 167–173):

> *Brasher went into the lead and I slipped in effortlessly behind him, feeling tremendously full of running. My legs seemed to meet no resistance at all. … We seemed to be going so slowly! … I was relaxing so much that my mind seemed almost detached from my body. There was no strain. … My mind took over. It raced well ahead of my body and drew my body compellingly forward. I felt that the moment of a lifetime had come. The world seemed to stand still, or did not exist. … I felt at that moment that it was my chance to do one thing supremely well. … I knew I had done it before I even heard the time.*

When we encounter experiences like this, we may think that the principle of "no pain, no gain" needs to be replaced with "no pain, maximum gain"—even in demanding endurance sports.

Peak experiences are not limited to sport. Here is the orchestra conductor Valery Gergiev, Artistic Director and Principal Conductor of the Kirov Ballet and Opera Company, in Saint Petersburg, Russia, describing the magical moments he has experienced during a performance (Harung, 1999, p. 55):

> *At 8 o'clock it starts. And you are silent. You look at the orchestra or your opera performers. Even in the darkness, they watch your eyes. You move your hands and the music begins and once in a great while you deliver something they cannot explain ... a truly world-class performance. It is moments like these which connect us human beings with the gods. It is magic.*

In whatever type of activity they occur, peak experiences have many appealing features: Joy, effortlessness, deep relaxation, and enhanced perception. We studied peak performers in sports, management, music, and a range of professions and compared them to average-performing controls. We found that most of the world-class performers and also most of the average performers reported such rewarding moments, in line with what is common. Thus, peak experiences are natural. They represent moments in which we tap into the deepest level of our latent mental potential. And the result is not simply a more pleasant subjective experience, but often dramatically improved performance.

Have you enjoyed such rewarding moments?

A Model for Excellence

Everyone seeks excellence in performance and happiness in life. However, performance is normally considered complicated to understand and difficult to improve. The reality revealed by research is that factors commonly thought to underlie top performance cannot explain greatness—factors like level of education, extent of practice, or the size of incentives. To illustrate, research on millions of adults in thousands of studies spanning up to 90 years shows that education accounts for only 1 percent of performance levels, work experience only 3 percent, and age in adults 0 percent (Schmidt and Hunter, 1998; Robertson and Smith, 2001).

Our model for excellence suggests that the secret of success in any profession or field of activity depends on the *single* factor of higher mind-brain development. We discovered this secret during our research on the peak performers and their controls. Mind-brain development includes a sequence of fundamental shifts in how we see ourselves, others, and the world—shifts which are based on refinements in brain functioning, including higher brain integration. Higher mind-brain development naturally expresses itself in higher performance in any profession, vocation, or organization.

This model of successful performance says that who we *are* is much more important than the knowledge, skills, relationships, and resources we *have* and the actions we *perform*. With higher mind-brain development, our knowledge and skills become more useful, our relationships become more enriching, resources become more easily available, and our actions become more effective. Figure 1.1 presents our performance model with its four dimensions:

1. Brain functioning—the level of orderliness and economy of brain functioning.

2. Individual psychology—the depth and breadth of mental and feeling functioning.

3. Peak experiences—the frequency and persistence of peak experiences.

4. Social context—the level of development of the organization and society in which the performer operates.

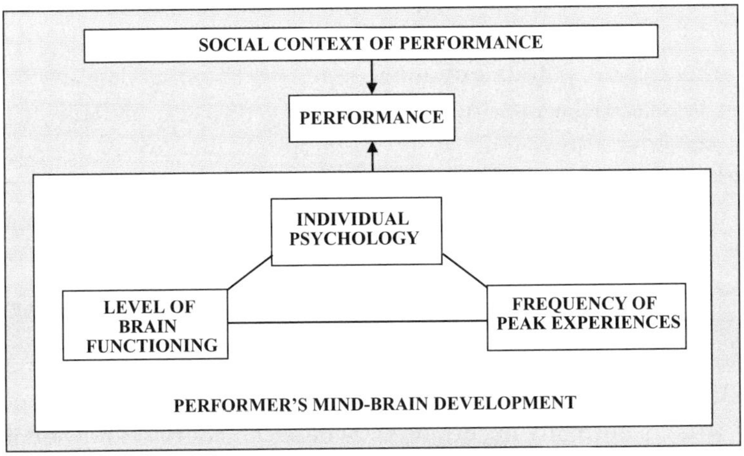

Figure 1.1 The Four Performance Dimensions

Unified Theory of Performance

Our Unified Theory of Performance (Harung and Travis, 2012; Travis et al., 2011; Harung, 2012) states that higher mind-brain development provides the basis of higher performance in any profession or field of activity. The level of performance can now be presented as a function f of:

$$\text{Performance level} \approx f\,(\text{level of brain functioning, individual psychology, frequency of peak experiences, social context of performance}) \qquad (1.1)$$

Mind-brain development includes the dynamic interplay of brain functioning, individual psychology, and peak experiences within the ever-changing social and environmental setting, as illustrated Figure 1.1. Research illustrates aspects of this interplay:

- *Between brain and psychology.* The brains of people with higher intelligence use up less sugar and transfer information faster and in a more dependable way than those of adults with average intelligence (Haier, 1993).
- *Between psychology and peak experiences.* The frequency of peak experiences triggered for the individual is significantly correlated with the degree of development of individual psychology (Panzarella, 1980).

Simplifying the Understanding of Performance

This book explores patterns of mind-brain functioning that we think are common to world-class performance in any profession or field of life. We will not consider knowledge, skills, and abilities that are particular to any one vocation or profession. Explaining performance through one primary factor—mind-brain development—simplifies the understanding of a complex field and makes it more feasible to implement major performance improvements in practice.

Mind-brain development has its range in commonly experienced stages of cognitive and moral development as well as in higher human development beyond what is normally experienced. Where can we find knowledge about the full range of human development? The Western discipline of psychology is useful, but it focuses on the development of individual psychology and personality, and often overlooks peak experiences. Most importantly, it does not provide effective techniques for spontaneously unfolding such experiences.

In contrast to the West, higher human development has been the primary focus in the Vedic tradition of knowledge in India for thousands of years. This tradition asserts that higher human development is completely natural, and offers techniques that individuals can use to systematically cultivate such development. Integrating knowledge from the East and West thus provides a true foundation for peak performance.

Mental Levels in the Vedic Tradition

> *I am asked where my work originates, and if I knew I would go there more often to find more.*
>
> — Arthur Miller, American author

Maharishi Mahesh Yogi (1969), world-leading expert in Vedic knowledge, describes the mind as a hierarchy of processing levels that determines what we perceive and how we respond to the environment. This model is shown in Table 1.1. Mind-brain development consists of uncovering progressively deeper mental levels. Deeper, more subjective levels guide and direct more expressed and objective levels. In this hierarchy, the most expressed levels are behavior and senses. Next are the levels of desires, which motivate action, and the thinking mind responsible for concrete thinking, memory, and associations. The intellect, the next deeper level, discriminates among the contents of the mind and decides what is right and what is wrong. The heart or feelings, the subsequent level, underlie and influence the directions the intellect takes. The ego is the core of the individual. Our individual ego integrates all the other mental levels into meaningful experiences. Finally, Transcendental Consciousness is the source of the individual mind. It is the reservoir of wakefulness, creativity, and intelligence that is expressed in our thoughts, choices, and actions.

Table 1.1 Levels of Mental Functioning from Outer Behavior to Inner Transcendental Consciousness

Behavior	Behavior
	Senses
	Desires
Lower self	Thinking mind
	Deciding intellect
	Feeling
	Ego: Individual "experiencer"
Higher Self	Transcendental Consciousness

The word *mind* has two meanings in this book: (1) the wholeness that includes all mental levels, and (2) the specific mental level that carries out thinking. It will be apparent from the context which meaning is appropriate.

The relation between the mind, the intellect, and the heart or feelings can be illustrated by a concrete situation. Your computer has broken down and you need to call the computer store. The mind is like an "open camera" that takes in relevant information: "What is the model of the computer? What is broken? Where is the computer store? What time is it?" The intellect next assesses the information in the mind: "Is it difficult to replace the defective part? Do I need to go to the store, or can they just send the part to me?" If you decide you need to go to the store, the next logical question might be, "Is it near rush hour, and if so should I go in the morning?" Meanwhile, the feelings are coloring your intellect-based choices. If you *feel* that you really want a new computer, you may decide that it is not cost-effective to repair the old one (even though this may not really be the case).

Intellect and feelings. The intellect works in a step-by-step fashion, tends to look for differences, and has a tendency to set things apart, which may easily result in opposition and conflicting interests. The feeling level, on the other hand, is contextual and instantaneous, and provides a refined value of discrimination. In addition, the heart has the ability to unite, harmonize, and bring things together, thereby complementing the intellect so that together they provide for more holistic and life-supportive thought, speech, and behavior.

Ego. The individual ego is the deepest level or core of one's personality. The ego feels through the heart, decides through the intellect, and sees through the eyes. It is the sense of "I," the knower or "experiencer." A note of explanation may be needed here since the word "ego" commonly refers to narrow-minded selfishness (egocentric). This negative meaning is appropriate at earlier stages of mind-brain development. However, higher growth expands the ego beyond the restrictions of individual personality to include more of the needs of others—one increasingly lives the saying that "the world is my family." With this development, the ego becomes progressively more comprehensive, problem-centered, self-forgetful, spontaneous, and trusting. *Ego-integration* (Loevinger, 1976) represents the fullest unfolding of individual ego, also called *self-realization* (Maslow, 1968).

Every person has all mental levels—it is just a matter of enlivening and integrating them. Progressive uncovering of deeper mental levels develops a better psychology, which now organize and integrate more expressed levels. This development thus enhances our motivation, perception, and thinking. The transition from an intellect-based to a feeling- or ego-based psychology brings with it many new attributes that can benefit performance, such as:

- From *extrinsic* motivation (winning, money, power, and fame) to *intrinsic* motivation (happiness, autonomy, mastery, and purpose).
- From reactive and treatment to proactive and preventive.
- From win-lose to win-win interpersonal strategies.
- From short-term to long-term perspectives.

Transcendental Consciousness, the most fundamental level, is experienced on its own when thinking and feeling settle down completely. Self-awareness is maintained without mental activity. Transcendental Consciousness is the most expanded or universal level of self-awareness, which is called the *higher Self* to distinguish it from the *lower self*. According to Maharishi (1969, p. 339), "The lower self is that aspect of the personality which deals only with the relative aspect of existence. It comprises the mind that thinks, the intellect that decides, the ego that experiences. ... The higher Self is that aspect of the personality which never changes. ... " The higher Self is the source of our thoughts and feelings, a state of restful alertness and bliss. Even though Transcendental Consciousness is there at the source of thought and underlying all active levels of individual mind, most people are not aware of it: "since [it] commonly remains in tune with the senses projecting outwards toward the [physical] realms of creation, the mind misses or fails to appreciate its own essential nature, just as the eyes are unable to see themselves" (Maharishi, [1963] 2001, p. 7).

Many of the qualities of Transcendental Consciousness, as defined by Maharishi, have been discussed in modern science as peak experiences, which Abraham Maslow described in terms of "going beyond and above selfhood," "transcendence of time and space," and "fusion with the world" (1968, p. 105 and p. 113; 1998, p. 42). During peaks, Transcendental Consciousness is experienced either on its own or coexisting with activity. Performance during a peak experience is characterized by bliss, inner calmness even amidst dynamic activity, effortlessness, spontaneous right action, freedom from fear, a sense of invincibility, and world-class performance. Pelé, generally regarded as the greatest soccer player of all time, describes a peak experience that includes feeling invincible during a world championship final that his team won (Pelé and Fish, 1977, p. 51):

> *Suddenly I felt a strange calmness I hadn't experienced in any of the other games. It was a type of euphoria; I felt I could run all day without tiring, and I could dribble through any of their team or all of them, that I could almost pass through them physically. I felt I could not be hurt. It was a very strange feeling and one I had never felt before. Perhaps it was merely confidence, but I have felt confident many times without that strange feeling of invincibility.*

Real success in outer behavior depends on using *all* levels of the mind. The power of the deepest levels—even in a physically tough endurance sport like cross-country skiing—is brought out by the following quote by Thomas Alsgaard:

> *Deeper [mental] aspects have much greater potential. Much, much greater potential. The intellect, [past] experience, and knowledge lie at the back of the head, in the unconscious. ... My experience after many years at the top is that there is a tremendous amount in the mental, a tremendous amount. My point of view is that this is what differentiates the best from the second best.*

Mind-brain Development and Age

Since mind-brain development is important for level of performance, it will be useful to consider how brain development is related to age.

1. CHILD DEVELOPMENT

At birth, brain cells are present, but they are not connected. In the first 25 years of life, biological information in the DNA (*nature*) interacts with life experience (*nurture*) to optimize the number of neural connections and the quality of those connections to support adult thinking and behavior. During childhood and youth we enjoy substantial mind-brain development.

2. ADULT DEVELOPMENT

While the process of brain maturation governed by DNA typically finishes in the early twenties (Roderick and Kilts, 2007), ongoing experience continues to change the brain throughout our life (Toga et al., 2006). Experience is thus the driver of brain development in adults. The brain is a living organ; it adapts to every experience throughout life. This ongoing adaptation is known as *neuroplasticity* (Fields and Stevens-Graham, 2002). As a consequence, 70 percent of our brain connections change every day (Segal, 2004). To use an analogy, the brain is a river and not a rock (Travis, 2012a). Each experience creates a wave of electrical activity over the brain that brings awareness of the inner and outer environment. At the same time, the brain connections activated by that experience become enhanced to more easily facilitate the same experience in the future. It is like walking down a path—with each usage it becomes progressively more likely and easy to again use the same path.

Neuroplasticity explains why brain development usually freezes in early adulthood. Since existing brain connections determine how we perceive the world and make choices, the experiences we choose will tend to simply strengthen current brain circuits. These well-used brain circuits then impel us to continue to think and act in the same way in the future. Thus, if we do not consciously seek out qualitatively different experiences, our brain will get into a habit of making the same choices over and over. Today, education and life are almost exclusively focused on the intellect and the more surface mental levels. Since the intellect dominates, mental concepts and categories tend to divide society, e.g., opposing political views, strong class differences, and strong religious ideologies.

However, music and the arts stimulate the feeling level, and may thus facilitate development that integrates the brain and harmonizes different systems of thought. To develop even further, the heart and ego need to be transcended. Ego-transcendence can occur during certain meditation practices that go beyond thought and mental control (see Chapter 7). Only with such interventions can the human condition expand beyond the current scenario—in which relatively few individuals display higher mind-brain functioning—and reach a state where Transcendental Consciousness and peak performance are generally available.

In contrast, in the absence in society of ego-transcendent experiences, significant mind-brain development seems to rarely occur after reaching adulthood. As a result, mental levels below the intellect—such as feelings—normally remain in darkness, affecting our thought and behavior in an unconscious way. Therefore, Transcendental Consciousness remains hidden to the general population. Fortunately, there is a highly positive side to this shortcoming since it implies a substantial potential for further growth in almost everybody. This suggests that the level of performance and happiness in society can be dramatically improved.

Mind-brain Development and Success: Four World-class Performance Studies

> *... someday there will undoubtedly be a science—it may be called the Science of Man—which will seek to learn more about man in general through the study of the creative man.*
>
> — Pablo Picasso, Spanish painter

In four studies, we have documented the relation between inner mind-brain development and outer success. These studies form the backbone of this book. The subjects and procedures of these four studies are outlined below. All subjects were above 25 years of age apart from the controls in study 1. The findings are introduced here and then discussed in detail later in the appropriate chapters.

1. WORLD-CLASS PERFORMERS IN A VARIETY OF PROFESSIONS

This pilot study examined the inner experiences, attitudes, work habits, and insights of a number of peak performers (The Performance Group, 1993; Harung et al., 1996). The subjects were people known internationally for their ability to achieve and maintain a position among the top performers in their areas of activity in business, government, sports, and education, as well as in creative areas such as the performing arts. They came from 16 countries from around the world. We measured the frequency of peak experiences in 22 such world-class performers as compared to students who had responded to the same questions. There was a significant difference between the two groups on two categories of peak experiences.

2. WORLD-CLASS ATHLETES

The first matched study investigated mind-brain development in top-performing Norwegian athletes (Harung et al., 2011). Working in collaboration with the National Olympic Training Centre in Norway (*Olympiatoppen*) and the Norwegian School for Sport Sciences (*Norges Idrettshøgskole*), 33 world-class athletes were selected and tested. The world-class athletes had placed among the top 10 in major global competitions (Olympic Games, world championships, and World Cup) for at least three different seasons. The 33 control athletes had been active in training and competing for at least three seasons but did not normally place amongst the top 50 percent in the Norwegian championships. The two groups were matched for gender, age, and type of sport. Levels of education were similar. The top athletes scored higher on brain integration (how coherent, restfully alert, and economical the functioning of the whole brain is), measures of better psychology (ego or self-development and moral reasoning), and speed of ignoring distractions.

3. TOP-LEVEL MANAGERS

In the second matched study, 20 Norwegian top-level managers were selected using a qualitative selection approach based on the following criteria: (1) successful leadership over 10 years or longer, (2) acting as a good example for others, and (3) broader perspective than just earning money, that is, exemplifying corporate social responsibility (Harung and Travis, 2012). The participating top-level managers had held their positions for an average of about 18 years. Sixteen were from the private sector and four from the public sector. Amongst those in the private sector, nine (56 percent) were successful entrepreneurs, and seven (44 percent) companies were listed on the Oslo Stock Exchange.

Controls were selected with limited management responsibilities (e.g., project manager, senior engineer, and product manager) or were skilled knowledge workers (e.g., associate professor, senior consultant, and programmer). They were matched for age, gender, level of education, and type of organization (private or public) with the top-level managers. Social mobility is high in Norway and given the matching, we think the low-level managers have had similar promotion opportunities to those of the top-level managers. The top-level managers scored significantly higher on all three measures of mind-brain development—brain integration, moral reasoning, and one category of peak experiences—while there was a trend for another peak experience question.

4. PROFESSIONAL CLASSICAL MUSICIANS

The third matched study compared 25 professional classical musicians with 25 amateur classical musicians (Travis et al., 2011). The professional musicians came from the Oslo Philharmonic Orchestra, the Norwegian Opera in Oslo, and the Gothenburg Symphony Orchestra. Enjoying a permanent position in a high-performing professional orchestra is subject to substantial international competition and strict and prolonged quality assurance through auditions and temporary engagements. The amateurs were playing in various amateur symphony orchestras in Oslo, the surrounding county of Akershus, or in Gothenburg. Both groups had been playing classical instruments since they were children. The two groups were matched for age and gender, and education levels were similar. The professional musicians scored higher on moral reasoning, three categories of peak experiences, a brain test of vigilance, and a measure of speed of mental processing.

Comprehensive View of Performance

The level of performance of the subjects and controls of the four peak performance studies were assessed in terms of performance quality or outer success. However, to provide a basis for the comprehensive perspective on performance outlined in this book, we will now introduce a broader performance model that consist of four aspects: Happiness generated for the performer, performance quality, societal benefits, and wealth generated.

1. HAPPINESS GENERATED FOR THE PERFORMER

In any performance, you should ask: How much happiness and mind-brain development does this performance create? Does it promote good health?

In the West, Aristotle (1998)—the great philosopher from ancient Greece—wrote that happiness is the natural goal of life. Maslow (1968, p. 73) identified peak experiences as "moments of highest happiness and fulfillment." Research has shown that the frequency of peak experiences is a good predictor of well-being, meaning, and purpose in life (Poloma and Pendleton, 1991). Anna Skogman, a violin player in the Norwegian Opera, said her performance was marked by "euphoria and lightness, and a strong desire to soon be allowed to play again!" The professional pianist Gonzalo Moreno from the Oslo Philharmonic Orchestra noted "... an incredible feeling of euphoria. I feel like the happiest person in the world." The cellist Johannes Martens from the Oslo Philharmonic Orchestra explained that after best performances he felt an "intense feeling of happiness and meaningfulness." The biathlonist Ole Einar Bjørndalen, the most decorated Winter Olympic athlete of all time, says, "I love to train. It is my hobby" (Haugli, 2014).

Happiness is primary also in Eastern models. According to Maharishi (1969, p. 62), "the very purpose of creation and of evolution is expansion of happiness." The Vedic tradition (Maharishi, 1986) identifies two kinds of happiness: Object-referral and self-referral:

- *Object-referral happiness* results from satisfying some specific need or desire, i.e., buying a new car or finding a new, nice place to go for a walk. This brings happiness, but it tends to be only temporary; after some time—one week or three months, sooner or later—the joy fades away. Local brain areas support object-referral happiness; when you eat an ice cream cone the pleasure center in your brain fires for a few minutes.

- *Self-referral happiness* is independent of objects. Self-referral happiness or bliss is related to the experience of Transcendental Consciousness. It is a lasting feature of a person—it is being happy without any particular reason. Hence, in general, the more familiar we are with Transcendental Consciousness, the more permanent bliss we have. Global brain integration supports self-referral happiness; when you feel blissful the brain works as an integrated whole, as suggested by total brain coherence.

Therefore, self-referral happiness is something one *is*; object-referral happiness is something one *has*. Different persons possess different degrees of self-referral happiness.

Stefan Klein is a German writer who formerly was the science editor of *Der Spiegel* magazine. In his popular book *The Happiness Formula* (2005), which has been translated into more than 20 languages, he notes that freedom and being in control of one's own life are two important factors for happiness. He continues, "People can be happy in almost all circumstances" (p. 265) and concludes that the external circumstances have less than 10 percent influence on our well-being. He also recognizes the relation between happiness and neurophysiological functioning: "Happiness is far more dependent on the way the brain perceives things, than on external circumstances" (p. 86). Klein concludes that "the most important thing you can do in the quest for happiness is therefore to know yourself" (p. 267). Since the key to happiness lies within, the person who compares himself or herself with others "has lost."

Self-referral happiness does not result from the sum of specific instances of object-referral happiness or satisfaction. Rather it grows as our inner sense-of-self deepens and the brain functioning becomes more refined. There is a strong connection between our moods and the amount of serotonin—a biochemical associated with self-esteem—in the brain (Duman et al., 1997). If we feel depressed, the level of serotonin drops and brain cells die. Conversely, positive emotions are associated with high levels of serotonin and new brain connections are more easily formed. Therefore, happiness may provide a "well of rejuvenation" for the brain.

There are many other benefits from greater happiness. Researchers have found that positive emotions—especially the awe we feel when touched by the beauty of nature, art, music, etc. —may give a boost to the body's defense system (Stellar et al., 2015). Life expectancy of people who report feeling most happy is 35 percent longer than of those who report feeling least happy (Steptoe and Wardle, 2011). Job satisfaction and happiness are good indicators of job performance (Gotvassli and Haugset, 2010). Persons higher in positive mood solve more problems, and specifically more with insight, compared with persons lower in positive mood (Subramaniam et al., 2009).

2. PERFORMANCE QUALITY

Quality is key in assessing level of performance. Performance can also be assessed in terms of breaking records, productivity, beauty, and user-friendliness. Abraham Maslow (quoted in Garfield, 1984, p. 154) describes top performance in these terms:

> *Greater efficiency, making an operation more neat, compact, simpler, faster, less expensive, turning out a better product, doing with less parts, a smaller number of operations, less clumsiness, less effort, more foolproof, safer, more "elegant," less laborious.*

Privett (1983, pp. 323–324) gives another description of peak performance:

> *Peak performance is identifiable and measurable and refers to a superior level of functioning, irrespective of type of activity. Peak performance is defined as superior behavior, operationally delineated as behavior that exceeds a person's average functioning. Peak performance is more efficient, creative, productive, or in some way better than ordinary behavior. Although the performance does not necessarily exceed that of other people, it surpasses what could be predicted for a person in a particular situation.*

3. SOCIETAL BENEFITS

We all live in a society and we all are responsible not only for the consequences our actions have on ourselves but also for their effects on others. In any performance, one should thus ask: How much happiness and mind-brain development does it create for *all* stakeholders? The stakeholders that need to be considered include the people who are affected, which in a business would include customers, suppliers, teams, the whole organization, the owner, the community, and society. As a consequence, a high level of performance is characterized by (1) behaving ethically, (2) nourishing others, the community, and society, (3) wasting as few resources as possible, (4) not creating undue pollution of the environment, and (5) being sustainable.

At first sight, one might think that exercising social responsibility and sustainability would decrease the financial performance of an organization. However, based on a matched sample of 180 companies that were compared on integrating social and environmental policies in their business model and operation, it was found that high-sustainability companies outperform low-sustainability companies (Eccles et al., 2011).

Even with a high level of self-referral happiness, we cannot be fully happy unless the people around us also are happy. With growing mind-brain development we will increasingly look to help others around us to grow as well. There is an intimate relationship between the individual and the social context in which he or she operates (Chapter 5). Just by becoming happier as an individual, we will therefore positively affect the happiness of those around us.

To create even more happiness around us, it is natural for us to work for the mind-brain development of others. Anwar el-Sadat, the former president of Egypt, won the Nobel Peace Prize for his pioneering work to create peace in the Middle East. The peak experiences he enjoyed as a young man, while in political prison, are the basis of the self-referral happiness that transformed his life. He observed how his own transformation naturally led him to work to increase the happiness of others (el-Sadat, 1979, pp. 79, 85, 86):

> *I was able to transcend the confines of time and place. ... Everything came to be a source of joy and delight. ... [T]his process of liberation ... contribute[s] to the achievement of perfect inner peace, and so provide[s] a man with absolute happiness. ... [From then on] my paramount object was to make people happy.*

4. WEALTH GENERATED

> *The use of quantity of money as a target has not been a success.*
>
> — Milton Friedman (2003), renowned Nobel laureate in economics

Money is today the dominant measure of level of performance. Money represents possibilities and resources that are essential for the performer, the organization, and other stakeholders to realize their goals. It can eliminate poverty and enhance our standard of living. Money also provides "energy" for investing in employees, new equipment, R&D, etc. Therefore, money is important. However, we have placed this factor last because money in itself does not guarantee happiness. In 1974, the University of Southern California economist Richard Easterlin concluded that it is only at the lowest levels of income that money makes a significant difference to subjective well-being; when the income is above the poverty limit, wealth has little effect on happiness (Argyle, 2001). Several research projects support the *Easterlin Paradox*. An interview of 50 of the richest Americans—each of whom was worth more than 100 million dollars—found that their satisfaction with life was little above average (Diener, 1985). Norway has a ten times higher GNP per capita than Costa Rica. Even so, the level of happiness in Costa Rica is almost the same (Gallup World Poll, 2010).

However, more comprehensive, recent research shows a relationship between income and happiness. A study at the University of Michigan analyzed data from 155 countries and found that subjective well-being rose along with income (Kluger, 2013). Another study analyzed the responses of over 800,000 people in 135 countries collected over a six-year period. It was found that income corresponds closely to happiness, but only if a person's wealth and aspirations keep pace. Psychologist Edward Diener at the University of Illinois concludes that money can boost happiness if it allows people to obtain more of the things they need and desire, but when their desires outpace what they can afford, even rising income can be accompanied by decreasing feelings of well-being. This underlies the importance of being self-referral to generate lasting happiness.

Our conclusion is that money can contribute to happiness, but that its importance is much exaggerated in current society. It is great to create wealth as long as the process (1) promotes happiness, health, and mind-brain development of those involved, and (2) is ethical, beneficial to society, and sustainable.

Examples of High and Low Performance

A few examples will illustrate the interplay among happiness, quality of work, societal benefits, and wealth generated in describing level of performance. A good symphony orchestra delivers high performance since it plays music that (1) creates happiness in each player, (2) is beautiful and of high quality, (3) creates happiness in the audience and is ethical and sustainable, and (4) generates an income. The same applies to any form of life-supportive entertainment and to education. For today's business world the situation is more mixed:

1. *Organizations that nourish society.* A survey of Norwegian CEOs found that 92 percent did *not* feel that there was a contradiction between giving the owners maximum return on investment and at the same time exercising environmental, ethical, and societal responsibility (Argument Gruppen, 2003). In fact, 91 percent of the CEOs felt that corporate social responsibility would *improve* the profitability of their business. Going green can lead to more innovation and greater value created. High-performing organizations tend to have a purpose beyond making money, e.g., to pioneer innovation of life-supporting products or services, and are often able to satisfy all stakeholders.

2. *Organizational that do not nourish society.* Some businesses provide useful goods or services to customers and create wealth for the owners. However, at the same time, they may underpay workers in developing countries, use child labor, or unduly pollute the environment. Such behavior reduces their overall level of performance. Other businesses may even have detrimental effects on society, such as those associated with the production of tobacco, arms, and violent films. For some such companies, the core idea seems unfortunately to be that if you make money, then everything is OK.

Overview of this Book

This book reveals the secret of high performance: Excellence in any profession, vocation, or organization primarily depends on the single factor of high mind-brain development. We may say that mind-brain development is the "active ingredient" in performance. Chapters 2–5 explore the four dimensions of mind-brain development: Enhanced brain functioning, better psychology, more frequent peak experiences, and higher organizational and societal development. Chapter 6 integrates these four dimensions and outlines the true basis of peak performance. Since high mind-brain development is essential for high performance, practical techniques for facilitating human growth are considered in Chapter 7. Chapter 8 concludes the book.

Chapter 2

First Performance Dimension: Enhancing Brain Functioning—Objective Foundation of World-class Performance

It seems to me that we are on the edge of a new leap into correlating our subjective lives with external objective indicators. I expect a tremendous leap forward in the study of the nervous system because of these new indications.

—Abraham Maslow (1971, p. 10)

Your brain is by far the most complex and sophisticated machinery in the universe. It contains over 100 billion neurons or brain cells. Each neuron is connected to at least 10,000 other neurons. The total number of connections is thus more than 1,000,000,000,000,000. Assuming that you count one number per second and that you count 24 hours a day, 7 days a week, it would take more than 30 million years for you to count all these connections. As a consequence of this vast number of cells and connections, the calculated number of possible signal paths in the brain is much larger than the number of elementary particles in the whole of the known universe (Storm, 2014).

Brain functioning underlies our thinking, speech, and action. You just turned the page. Your hand moved smoothly with no wasted effort. How did you do it? Your desire to see the next page was translated into signals from your brain that moved your hand. We see the world; we evaluate our experience; we respond to the world through brain functioning. Our brain is our link with the world. The quality of our brain connections determines the quality of perception. Is it a string or a snake? Is it a challenge or a stress? This is determined by brain functioning.

Two Parallel Paths of Processing in the Brain

All experience goes through two parallel paths in the brain—the *low road* and the *high road* responses. In Figure 2.1 the *low road* path is represented by a solid line, and the *high road* path is represented by a dotted line:

- The *low road* response uses lower brain structures such as the brain stem and the limbic system (part of the brain that controls our emotions), leading to a fast, automatic emotional response to the experience. This emotional response is sometimes called the "heart" response, though it is really driven by brain processes. This fast emotional response forms the background for evaluating the details of the experience, which are generated by the *high road* response.

- The *high road* response uses the cerebral cortex—the brain's outer layer—to determine the details of an experience and to reflect on and evaluate the details of the experience. The high road response is slower, and we are aware of each step of processing so we can make changes underway if necessary. These two outputs end up in the prefrontal cortex (frontal brain area behind the forehead, often called the CEO of the brain), which makes meaning of the details of the experience in light of the emotional response.

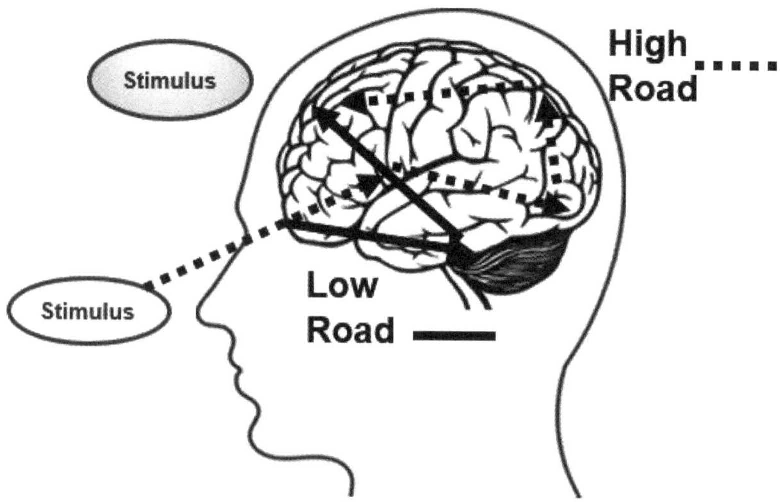

Figure 2.1 Brain and the Low and High Road of Processing Information

The low road response is faster because there are no decisions involved, just instinct and reflexive responses. The high road response is slower because it involves multiple decision-points to consider how the current experience relates with past experiences, current ideas, and future plans. Notice that we do not see the world as it is. Rather we see the world colored by our emotional responses. This is indicated in Figure 2.1 as the stimulus in the open oval, representing the world as it is, and the stimulus in the shaded oval, representing the effects of emotional tone on coloring our experience.

Higher mind-brain development enhances performance ability in two ways. First, the low road responses are less governed by biases and past experiences—especially stressful ones—allowing the performer to take a fresh look at the situation. Second, the whole brain—including the two roads—is more integrated, allowing performers to make better choices through a synergy of hunches and facts.

The following quote describes the interplay of the low road response—often identified as fine feeling, a hunch, or intuition (said to be from the heart), and the high road response—critical thinking and evaluation of an experience (Harung, 1999, p. 86):

> *My father said that if you must make decisions and not make mistakes, you must listen with your heart and soul. I asked him how that is possible, and he said you must get your first influence and answer from inside your heart. After three or four seconds your brain starts to analyze, to influence your decision. Your heart and soul answer must be first. If you do not manage this, you can go wrong.*
>
> — Mariss Jansons, a world-class Latvian conductor, son of the renowned conductor Arvīds Jansons

Overall Style of Brain Functioning is Key

Different parts of the brain carry out different tasks. Our research suggests that the *overall* or *global style* of functioning of the immense complexity of brain cells is the key to peak performance. Optimal performance therefore rests on optimal brain functioning. It is that simple. It is not mysterious. If your brain is functioning in a fragmented way then you only see differences. If your brain is functioning in an integrated way, the information from any one brain area is available to all brain areas. Then you will see the bigger picture that connects the parts. Enhanced brain functioning is measured by brain integration, which reflects the ability of the brain to integrate localized processing into a larger picture.

Research shows that the level of brain integration correlates positively with greater creativity, higher emotional stability, greater moral reasoning, more openness to experience, and lower anxiety (Travis et al., 2004). As seen in our studies of world-class performers, an integrated brain supports higher levels of mind-brain development, creative problem-solving, rewarding social interactions, high quality of life, and personal and professional success.

Different Types of Brain Waves

In 1924, the German psychiatrist Hans Berger made the first recording of the electrical waves produced when the brain functions. This technology is called EEG or electroencephalography. Berger placed two sensors on his son's head: One on the forehead and one on the back of the head. When his son was relaxing, Berger saw brain waves moving up and down at 8–13 cycles per second or Hz. He called these alpha waves. When his son opened his eyes, Berger saw brain waves going up and down at 16–20 cycles per second. These waves are called beta1. Since then other brain wave frequencies have been identified during sleeping and dreaming and during other cognitive tasks.

Table 2.1 shows the different EEG brain wave frequencies. As seen, sleep is associated with the slowest brain waves, delta. During delta activity, the brain is disconnected from the outside world and repairs the wear and tear of waking experience. The next higher frequency band, theta, is seen when we are dreaming (theta1) and when we are engaged in inner mental work, such as memory processes (theta2).

The next higher frequency band, alpha, also has two divisions. Alpha1 is seen when awareness is turned *within* and one is awake, and is associated with Transcendental Consciousness. Alpha2 is found when brain areas are "idling": Brain areas are primed and ready to act, but are not involved in processing experience. The next frequency band, sigma, is the marker of sleep onset. The highest frequency bands, beta and gamma, are present when the mind is focused on *outer* objects. Thus, the frequency of the brain waves indicates the type of mental functioning that is taking place.

Table 2.1 Brain Waves and Cognitive Processes

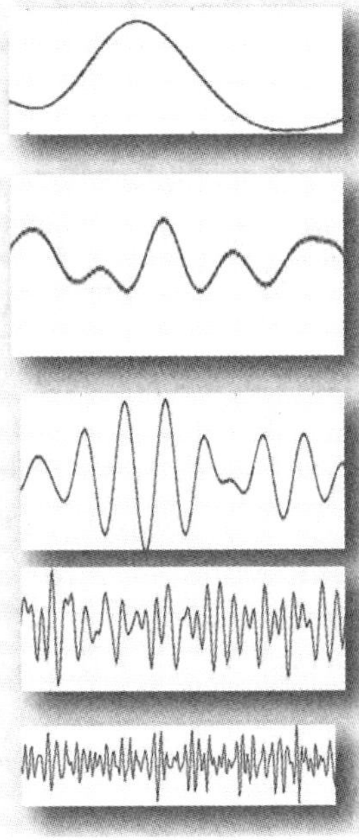

Frequency (cycles/sec or Hz)	Cognitive Processes
1-4 Delta	Restoration during deep sleep
4-6 Theta1	Drowsiness and dreaming
6-8 Theta2	Inner mental processes such as during a memory task
8-10 Alpha1	Inner wakefulness
10-13 Alpha2	Brain modules primed to be used in a task, but currently quiet
13-16 Sigma	Sleep onset
16-20 Beta1	Ongoing processing of experience
20-30 Beta2	Focus or concentration
30-50 Gamma	Strong focus or concentration

Brain Integration Scale

The Brain Integration Scale, which we have developed, indexes whether the brain is working as an integrated whole or is functioning in fragmented parts. By analogy, imagine you are sitting in the Sydney Opera House. Each player is warming up and the orchestra as a whole is producing unpleasant, disconnected noise. Once the conductor enters the stage, the players perform together in an integrated way and you can enjoy the harmony of the musical piece.

The conductor in the brain is the *prefrontal cortex*. The prefrontal cortex directs the rest of the brain in a fashion similar to how a CEO directs his or her organization. Frontal brain areas have physical connections with all other brain areas. This high level of physical connections supports the role of the prefrontal cortex in planning, decision-making, impulse control, and other higher cognitive functioning. The prefrontal cortex integrates the concrete present with past memories, emotions, values, plans, and goals, and determines our next step.

Greater integration of the functioning of the prefrontal cortex, as measured by coherence, is one component of higher brain integration. Another component is wakefulness and broader awareness, as measured by alpha amplitude. The last component is the efficiency and timeliness of resource allocation, as measured by how the brain prepares for action. The Brain Integration Scale provides an objective measure to allow performers and managers/mentors/coaches to monitor the level and growth of brain refinement. With higher brain integration, one can be successful in increasing challenging situations. Thus, higher brain integration raises one's performance capacity. The three components of the Brain Integration Scale are calculated from brain waves during demanding computer tasks.

1. COHERENT FUNCTIONING

Different brain areas carry out different functions, e.g., the back of the brain processes sensory input, the middle directs motor functioning, and as seen, the front coordinates all other brain areas. Coherence means that waves from different parts of the brain are firing in a synchronized way. The Brain Integration Scale uses coherence across a wide range of frequencies, 6–40 Hz, called *broadband* coherence. Broadband coherence in the prefrontal cortex suggests global integration of the whole brain.

If the CEO is absent from a company, the different departments are not coordinated: The sales department sells goods it does not have; the production department manufactures objects that there is no market for. If the CEO is present, then it is his or her job to see that each action is integrated with the company's vision and goals and with the market and economic situation, and to decide upon synchronized organization-wide action. Similarly, when the brain's executive system is well integrated then all the different brain areas involved in experience and decision-making work as one, resulting in higher performance. This is why broadband frontal coherence is part of the Brain Integration Scale.

Two studies by other researchers support a relationship between brain coherence and higher performance. David A. Waldman and his colleagues at Arizona State University reported that higher coherence in the right frontal regions of the brain was found in participants who were assessed as high on inspirational/charismatic leadership (Waldman et al., 2011). In addition, a study at Massachusetts Institute of Technology found that synchronized brain waves enable rapid learning—neurons that hum together encode new information more efficiently (Antzoulatos and Miller, 2014).

2. BROAD AWARENESS

Different mental processing styles are marked by different brain patterns. Broad awareness is characterized by higher alpha1 and lower gamma waves. Alpha1 is seen during self-referral activities when awareness is turned within and we are highly awake. In contrast, gamma waves characterizes object-referral activity when attention is identified with outer objects; your experience is dominated by the immediate situation, and the larger picture is in the background or out of sight.

Higher alpha1 activity and lower gamma activity during tasks thus indicates that the person is at a balance point—being calm and alert at the same time. Then that person processes experience more in terms of an inner locus of control and is able to keep the big picture while focusing on the part. Greater inner balance allows us to be more adaptable to changes in, for example, associates, customers, competitors, market, technology, and economy.

3. EFFICIENT AND TIMELY ALLOCATION OF RESOURCES

The timing of brain processes is measured during simple and choice reaction-time tests. The simple reaction-time task measures how fast you respond to a single stimulus; the choice reaction-time task measures whether you remain balanced until you receive the necessary information to respond in one of two ways. Timely behavior means that you mobilize resources when needed and relax when they are not needed. Measuring the timing of brain activation provides an objective measure of efficiency and economy of brain processes.

Economy of brain processes as part of the Brain Integration Scale reflects the law of least action in physics. According to this principle of economy, all processes in the physical world spontaneously function with minimal expenditure of time, energy, and other resources (Hagelin, 1987). This principle describes the flow of a stream down a hillside and the loss of energy from a heated building. Similarly, a better match between task demands and brain activation is evident in more efficient behavior and fewer wasted resources. This is the basis for success.

Top Performers Have Higher Brain Integration

We assessed levels of Brain Integration Scale scores in world-class athletes, top-level managers, and professional classical musicians, and compared to matched average-performing controls.

I. WORLD-CLASS ATHLETES

We found significant differences between the top athletes and average-performing controls on the Brain Integration Scale (Harung et al., 2011). In addition, the 33 top athletes habituated much faster to a loud sound, which means that they more quickly stopped reacting to irrelevant distractions.

Higher brain integration. Figure 2.2 presents the typical brain coherence for one world-class and one control athlete. In these coherence maps, the nodes represent the standardized points where the electrodes are placed on the scalp, and a line between two points means that the electrical waves at each end are at least 70 percent in coherence with each other. The darker the line is, the higher the coherence. The higher coherence in the top performer is evident from the larger number of lines between the points.

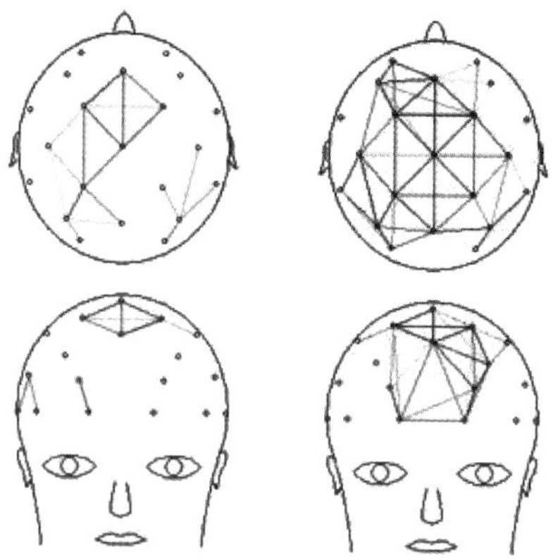

Figure 2.2 Brain Coherence Map for Typical World-class Athlete and Control

The lines signify that the brain waves in the two adjoining points are more than 70 percent coherent with each other—the thicker the line, the larger the coherence. In the world-class athlete (right) the electrical brain wave activity in different parts of the brain is more coherent than in the control (left).

Higher brain integration scores by the top athletes suggest that they were more economical in their response; they were better at mobilizing brain resources or relaxing depending on the demands of the situation. Many sports involve complex reactions, and this finding has profound implications for athletic performance. Consider tennis, for example, where you as a player have to make a decision about your next move in the time span between when your opponent hits the ball and when the ball gets to you. Let us assume that you are able to wait longer than your opponent before deciding on your next move. Ideally, you wait until the very instant when you are going to hit the ball. This delay will give you a competitive edge, because you are most up-to-date on your opponent's position and motion and can direct your ball in the most effective way. Roger Federer, considered one of the greatest tennis players of all time, is said to be able to wait until the very last moment before he commits to a shot. Therefore, the ability to stay restfully alert as long as possible before acting may to a considerable extent explain the difference between peak and average performers in many sports.

The high brain integration in top athletes is translated into strain-free, harmonious, and effective action during a peak experience. Tutko and Tosi (1976, p. 105) have described this rewarding experience as follows:

> *You are physically free. Your body is able to move naturally, seemingly on its own, unhampered by tensions. You may at the time even have been surprised at your own strength, speed, or agility, even though there was no strain. … You are in harmony. No part of you conflicts with another. Mind and body work together. You are moving with the action and have the feeling of being one with it.*

Faster habituation to irrelevant sound. The world-class athletes habituated—stopped responding—to an irrelevant tone much faster than the controls. Fast habituation rates reflect higher neural efficiency. The efficient physiology responds initially to any novel stimulus, but then stops responding once the stimulus is recognized as being non-threatening or irrelevant. The top performers habituated about three times faster than the controls. Thus the top performers were better able to ignore distractions and focus on what was important for success.

Prefrontal brain areas control habituation to stressful stimuli. Higher prefrontal coherence would be expected to lead to faster habituation, as was seen in these data. Faster habituation by high-performing athletes may explain their frequently described experience of the *tunnel*. In the tunnel, which is often related to high performance, the athletes are able to focus only on factors relevant to their successful performance, and exclude irrelevant input, e.g., irrelevant thoughts of the past, present, and future, and irrelevant input from competitors, audience, and the environment. The tunnel effect may reflect natural habituation, which is automatic and does not require conscious, effortful control.

Katrine Lunde, a high-performing female handball goalkeeper, says she depends on being in the "bubble" for performing at her best. Then everything other than the game is locked out and there is no other place to be that she enjoys more (Hole, 2013).

Sport conducted at the highest level is comprised of high expectations and high levels of perceived stress. Therefore, it is of vital importance that the athletes are able to cope with this situation (Pensgaard and Roberts, 2000). The ability to stay calm and focused becomes essential, and any elevated tension—either psychological or physiological—might interfere with a fine-tuned technique. Thus, the combination of more rapid habituation and higher brain integration (which correlates with low levels of anxiety) seems particularly useful at the highest level of competitive sport.

2. TOP-LEVEL MANAGERS

> *It would be a world sensation if one found a neurobiological basis for why some people are good leaders.*
>
> — Dr Jan Ketil Arnulf (2009),
> Norwegian School of Management

Until now, leadership has been studied almost exclusively in terms of psychology and behavior. In contrast, our research with Norwegian top-level managers found that their brain integration was significantly higher than that of low-level managers (Harung and Travis, 2012)—adding a new dimension to the foundation of effective leadership. Our brain data provide a holistic, objective, and neurophysiologic perspective to the discussion of more effective versus less effective managers. Greater brain integration may serve as the global context to better integrate localized brain functioning. While different management styles may be beneficial in different situations, higher levels of brain integration could provide a *common* basis for more integrated and effective perception, planning, action, and evaluation in *all* situations.

Enhancing mind-brain development—as reflected in more integrated brain waves—could thus activate more comprehensive perspectives and strategies, enabling managers and associates to see beyond immediate circumstances and deal with larger principles and forces at work in the marketplace and in society. This expanded perspective could guide cognitive, behavioral, and organizational strategies and execution for greater success in business and industry.

Due to such factors as globalization, new technology, fluctuating markets, and high speed of change, business management is a highly complex and dynamic profession. High brain integration may therefore be useful for leadership success since it illustrates efficient integration of strategy and implementation, and of theory and practice. There are specific benefits for managers related to higher scores on each of the three components of the Brain Integration Scale:

1. Higher frontal coherence indicates improved integration of different areas of the brain which have different responsibilities and carry out different functions. A more coherent brain could therefore explain the important integration of heart and mind, which comes with higher human development. Higher brain coherence could also enable managers to act with integrity—integrating thought, speech, and action—so that they say what they do and do what they say—"walk the talk."

2. Intuition implies knowing something directly from within, without or with little use of objective facts and sensory impressions. Being intuitive depends on our ability to notice subtle signals in the brain. This requires that we quiet the overall activation of the brain. The enhanced restful alertness corresponding to high alpha/gamma ratios can enable the leader to be more open to intuitions that provide early and vital signals/warnings of important changes in employees, markets, technology, and governmental policies. The combination of greater coherence and enhanced wakefulness may also enable total management, which integrates the manager, managing, and managed into a comprehensive whole (Harung, 1999).

   One top-level manager we studied reported how an intuitive experience spontaneously gave him important insights:

> *A feeling that thoughts float, find their own ways, and I let them float. I have experienced that in such situations formerly unthought-of solutions or alternatives pop up. Also "warning signs" have popped up in such situations, warnings that later have proven to be very correct.*

3. Mobilizing resources when needed is key for effective management, which aims at doing less and accomplishing more. Managers endeavor to *maximize* quality, productivity, customer satisfaction, employee satisfaction, profit, and shareholder value while they *minimize* the expenditure of human resources, natural resources, time, money, and other resources (e.g., lean management and just-in-time production). More economical brain functioning may underlie this type of managerial behavior, increasingly enabling us to act in accordance with the law of least action whereby the simplest is most effective.

3. PROFESSIONAL CLASSICAL MUSICIANS

The third matched study compared 25 professional classical musicians from the Oslo Philharmonic Orchestra, the Norwegian Opera, and the Gothenburg Symphony Orchestra with amateur classical musicians from the Oslo and Gothenburg regions (Travis et al., 2011). The professional musicians scored higher on moral reasoning, three categories of peak experiences, and on two vigilance tests. To our surprise, in terms of brain integration, *both* the professional and amateur musicians scored on the level of the world-class athletes and top-level managers.

Extensive musical experience during childhood, a time of massive cortical reorganization, shapes brain connections that continue into adulthood. For example, childhood musical experience enhances visual-spatial, verbal, and mathematical performance in adults (Hyde et al., 2009). Similar scores on the Brain Integration Scale may thus reflect the fact that both groups of musicians had played an instrument since childhood. Similar scores could also reflect that both groups had professional positions—the amateur musicians were effective in both their vocation (professional job) and avocation (music).

A high score on all three aspects of the Brain Integration Scale seems to be important for playing music in an orchestra:

1. Higher frontal coherence may underlie the ability to integrate brain areas involved in the diverse demands of musical performance. For instance, playing an instrument in an ensemble requires the brain to choose what is relevant in a complex situation including reading or remembering a score, timing issues, and coordination with other musicians. Coherence between different parts of the brain may underlie the player's experience of connectedness with the music and the environment. In a study of musicians, one of the subjects reported, "I felt exhilaration, release, joyous, being at one with the music and not only with the music but with the people, concert hall, etc." (Panzarella, 1980).

2. Restful alertness is essential for picking up minute changes in the musical movement of the orchestra.

3. Economy of action may help sustain wakefulness throughout a demanding concert lasting up to two hours. The players are able to rest between sections and be highly focused when they play.

Stress and Performance

In athletes or musicians, stress breaks down the smooth motion gained from extensive practice. Practice takes a complex sequence of responses, such as returning a 210 km/h tennis serve or playing many notes, chunks them together and stores them in the part of the brain associated with muscle memory, called the *basal ganglia*. You watch a gymnast on the high bar, doing all the incredible twisting and turning moves. If you ask her how she does each one, she will not be able to tell you. Her brain has chunked the movements together, and her basal ganglia makes her movements *automatic*. Stress stops smooth motor output. The muscles are tight and the attention focuses on only one part of the experience. The learned response is disrupted.

Faced with high levels of stress, executives may overreact to life experiences, become more irritable, and function in a more primitive and less reasoned way. They may lack the capacity to recognize problems or exploit possibilities. High levels of stress cause excessive wear and tear on the minds and bodies of leaders and their associates.

Stress versus challenge. It is vital to distinguish between stress and challenge. Some people say that they need "stress" to function at their best—that under "stress" they are more creative and energetic. However, they are probably talking about the enhancing effects of challenge rather than the debilitating effects of stress. Under challenge, the brain stem floods the brain with the biochemical *noradrenalin*. Noradrenalin speeds up all brain processing: The sensory areas perceive more clearly and distinguish finer details. The motor system is primed to go. The frontal executive areas are functioning faster. Challenge thus supports optimal performance.

But when the challenge gets *too high* and we feel that we cannot cope, the brain downshifts into a stress response. Under stress, an almond-sized structure deep in the brain, called the *amygdala*, fires rapidly. The amygdala adds emotions to experiences. It is part of fear conditioning and activates the "fight-or-flight" response. Now, the immediate sensory experiences (processed in the back of the brain) dominate. The frontal executive areas are turned off and a response dominated by fear is initiated. Since the frontal areas—which are responsible for the broad awareness essential for success in performance—are not available, we stop seeing the big picture. Behavior with the prefrontal cortex off-line is thus like a company whose CEO has suddenly disappeared, and it is unlikely that top organizational performance will result!

When stressed, we are gripped by our negative emotions and cannot see a solution. This behavior is appropriate if we're in a truly dangerous situation: If your car starts skidding at 100 km/h toward the ditch, you don't need to reflect on the feeling of skidding or on life in general—you need to focus sharply and respond immediately. When you're under stress, the fight-or-flight response hinders your ability to consider long-range implications. Chronic stress can in fact cause the loss of brain volume, a condition that contributes to both emotional and cognitive impairment (Kang et al., 2012).

This book discusses how higher mind-brain development enhances frontal functioning and so buffers the effects of stress on brain functioning and behavior. Such development makes more inner resources available so that negative stressful situations are increasingly handled as positive challenges.

Neuroplasticity and Brain Integration

> *Every thought and experience is imprinted in physical form in the structure and functioning of the nervous system.*
>
> — Buonomano and Merzenich (1998)

How can we improve brain integration to improve our performance? Up until 20 years ago neuroscientists thought that brain connections were fixed after early childhood, so it was difficult later in life to make changes in brain functioning. However, recent breakthroughs in research in neuroplasticity demonstrate that the brain is changing with *every* experience, throughout our lives. Neuroplasticity thus provides a continuous mechanism for improving brain functioning so that we can realize the enormous latent potential that all of us have.

Through repeated practice and experience we create and strengthen neural circuits that support the smooth, automatic flow of thought and behavior. Neuroplasticity includes both increasing the number of connections between the neurons and increasing the *myelin* sheath around the axons (output fibers from the neurons). Myelin is a fatty substance that greatly increases the speed of transferring information. When we practice positive habits of thought and behavior, we may strengthen those brain circuits that allow us to excel in the changing professional and life environment. However, when we practice bad habits, we reinforce those circuits, and our bad habits continue and may even be strengthened.

This is a critical point to fully understand. Your choice of a specific profession or activity is also a choice of underlying brain circuits. For example, the brains of experienced taxi drivers in London were compared to those of beginners. It was found that experienced drivers had richer connections and therefore thicker brain areas in those parts of the brain associated with success at taxi driving, e.g., sense of direction, planning alternate routes, and reacting to obstruction in the road (Maguire et al., 2006). The brain area that represents the left hand in violin players—the hand that makes the chords—is eight times larger than the brain area that represents the right hand. Thus, the health of your brain isn't, as experts once thought, just the product of genetics and childhood experiences; it reflects your adult choices and experiences as well. Since every activity leaves its signature in the brain, every performer should ask, "What choices am I making? What am I doing?"

Reinforcing Habitual Brain Circuits

Current brain circuits determine how we perceive a situation and the choices we make; those choices lead to specific experiences that reinforce the brain circuits used. Thus, it is possible to get into a rut or bad habit whereby you reinforce your current brain circuits and your current level of brain integration, and do not continue to grow. This may explain why major brain refinements are found to be rare after late adolescence—after natural, biologically programmed brain maturation during growing up has ceased. A correlation of age versus brain integration in both the adult general population in our database (N=208) and in our three peak performance studies (N=142) showed that age explains less than 1 percent of variations in brain integration. More important, stressful experiences may in fact decrease levels of brain integration, as found in college students over the course of one semester (Travis et al., 2009).

How can we break out of the habit of reinforcing current brain circuits and fundamentally enhance brain integration across the lifespan? To achieve this, we need to seek out *new* experiences in kind rather than number; new experiences that require an expanded frame of reference; new experiences that explore inner consciousness rather than outer objects. Chapter 7 discusses how meditation practice can lead to continuous improvement in brain integration throughout life by allowing the mind to access Transcendental Consciousness, the most expanded mental level.

Summarizing this Chapter

This chapter lays the foundation for the book by describing the essential role the brain physiology plays in improved performance. Using the Brain Integration Scale—a measure of the enhanced functioning of the *whole* brain—we have shown that high performance is associated with a coherent, alert, and economical brain. A major scientific breakthrough in recent years is neuroplasticity, which means that the brain is constantly changing throughout life. Neuroplasticity provides a practical mechanism for you to continue to shape your brain in a desired direction, and consequently to change to higher performance. The next chapter will describe how enhanced brain functioning leads to better psychology and thereby increases your capacity for performance.

Brain integration is one of the performance dimensions because the functioning of this highly complex and sophisticated machinery underlies mental processes that are critical for peak performance. However, excellence naturally also depends on the optimal functioning of the whole body: Sound health is therefore described in Chapter 7. Since the brain is primary for excellence, we can appreciate the American inventor Thomas Edison when he writes that the chief function of your body is to carry your brain around.

Chapter 3

Second Performance Dimension: Better Psychology—Getting to Effective Performance

All true greatness must come from internal growth.

— *Ralph Waldo Emerson, American author*

What drives peak performers? Let us consider an extraordinary runner in *biathlon*, a popular and entertaining winter sport that alternates between cross-country skiing (dynamic action, endurance, and mind-body coordination) and rifle shooting (relaxation, focus, and precision). When Ole Einar Bjørndalen placed second in the Vancouver Winter Olympics, he said, "Medals don't mean anything" (Haugli, 2010). The article went on to say that Ole Einar does not collect medals, he collects good races—and this he felt he had accomplished during this particular race. Ole Einar should know what he is talking about: He is the most decorated Winter Olympics athlete of all time! His last two gold medals he won in the Sochi Olympics at the age of 40, making him the oldest individual winter gold medal winner ever. As of March 2015, he has won 27 gold, 16 silver, and 10 bronze medals in Olympic Games or world championships—a total of 53 medals. No wonder Bjørndalen is often referred to by the nickname "The King of Biathlon."

Even so, Ole Einar thinks he is still not perfect as a biathlonist: "No, I don't feel like that, but I have approached [perfection] during recent years." Seeking perfection, he is still passionately concerned with further developing his training methods, skis, and equipment. He made a comeback in 2014 after a couple of years with not-so-brilliant performances. After winning his first Sochi gold medal, he said on Norwegian TV2 that the most important thing was not winning the gold medal, but that he had been able to make a comeback. It is apparent that Ole Einar is driven by intrinsic motivation—he is primarily competing against himself—a feature that is often found in peak performers and that naturally belongs to a better psychology.

The American speed skater Eric Hayden, who won all five gold medals during the Lake Placid Olympics in 1980, also demonstrated inner motivation when he forgot his medals and left them in a drawer in his hotel room upon leaving the Games. The cross-country skier Marit Bjørgen is the woman with the most medals in Winter Olympics, but after winning three gold medals in Sochi in 2014, she said in an interview with the newspaper *Aftenposten* that she did not think about how many medals she had won.

Cultivating a better psychology—psychological development—is the dimension of human growth commonly researched and described by Western psychology. This dimension progressively uncovers deeper mental levels: The thinking mind, the deciding intellect, feelings, and the experiencing ego, as shown in Table 1.1. The post-conventional domain corresponds to acting from the deeper levels of feelings and ego. Some authors seem to include post-conventional experiences in peak experiences, which are based on transcendence (see Chapter 4). We distinguish between the two classes. In this chapter, we present a number of characteristics related to the post-conventional domain and the resulting high performance. Post-conventional characteristics are discussed in two categories:

1. *Temporary* post-conventional *experiences,* usually occurring during high performance, e.g., greater wholeness and sharp focus. For completeness, we also mention a more general experience called *flow*.

2. *Lasting* post-conventional *traits* that we found expressed in the day-to-day life of the world-class performers, for example, self-reliance and growth-orientation.

This chapter ends with an overview of the theory of psychological development. The major accomplishments of the world-class athletes quoted in this book are summarized in Appendix 2.

Post-conventional Experiences during High Performance

We interviewed the world-class athletes and controls about their temporary experiences *during* their best competitions. We asked them (Boes et al., 2014, p. 424):

> *I would like you to describe what happens when you perform at your very best. Please describe the specific situation, your inner experiences*

> *in body and mind, and how you relate externally to others and the environment during optimal performance. You may also want to talk about what happens before and after such instances.*

Content analysis of the interviews found greater wholeness in the top athletes (Boes et al., 2014). In addition, responses on the self-report questionnaire of peak experiences from athletes, managers, and musicians revealed qualities of sharp focus, refined perception, enhanced intuition, increased inner silence, and greater happiness.

1. GREATER WHOLENESS

A feeling of wholeness or the "total picture" during high performance was reported by several top athletes. This experience—which was described using words like *wholeness, boundary breaking, free of limitations, oneness,* and *wide-angle perception*—appears to help organize and guide the overall strategy used to achieve the athletes' goals. Thomas Alsgaard says:

> *I am after the wholeness. Generally speaking, I have this feeling of wholeness. The small details are rather unessential. It is the total picture and wholeness that is important. It is this wholeness I have been feeling and looking for. If this wholeness is there, you may say that things work out well. ... But I am so relaxed. ... [The body] moves easily. Reduced friction, but everything is connected together here. The body feeling light is also a long process; the body does not become this by itself. There's a lot of psychology, not only physical training.*

Recall that brain integration was significantly higher in top-performing athletes and managers than in controls. It is likely that the subjective feeling of wholeness and expanded awareness has its basis in high brain integration. Bjørn Rune Gjelsten is a male offshore boat racer who won a record five class 1 powerboat World Cups and who also is a highly successful businessman. An experience in the direction of such wholeness is expressed when he talks about his best performances:

> *It is a different state of mind, the great picture, beyond time. The intellect is disconnected—it lies in the background. Performance is characterized by spontaneity and automation. It's very strange. I become part of the boat, feel a union with the boat. An extreme feeling where there is wholeness: We [Gjelsten and his engineer], boat, and water.*

2. SHARP FOCUS

Our professional classical musicians illustrate the importance of focus for top performance. Christian Stene, principal clarinetist in the Norwegian Opera Orchestra, says, "Everything external is shut out. Only the concert podium and my colleagues are in the picture. I feel inspired and want to show what I can do with the music. I sound good and am in a way superior." The cellist Katharina Hager-Saltnes reports that during optimal performance "The mind is 100 percent in the music. No other thoughts." The bass opera singer Carsten Stabell in the Norwegian Opera noted:

> *During optimal performance I relate purely professionally to everything on the outside, meaning that all forms of signals from conductor, orchestra, pianist, or colleagues on stage are registered and interpreted in the matter of milliseconds. All interruptions from the outside are neglected.*

3. REFINED PERCEPTION

Bjørn Rune Gjelsten recollects how his perception became more refined during one of his best boat races:

> *There were vibrations in the boat—vibrations in several places. I perceived a signal that things were not OK. Afterwards, the black box showed vibrations in the 12th or 13th round. They were extremely small. … The senses were extremely stimulated: expanded wakefulness. I had a good feeling: exhilaration. It builds up as I am approaching the competition and lasts longer than the finish. There are phases of stepping down, all the way until bedtime, also next morning.*

Heidi Tjugum is a female handball goalkeeper who was part of the Norwegian team that won one world championship, one European championship, two European Cups, and a number of silver and bronze medals in such championships. Heidi reports on refined perception—and joy and beauty—during what seems to be a post-conventional experience:

> *I feel a security, warmness. The colors become pretty; the flag is beautiful. Yes, just joy, plainly speaking. There is a glorification. I experience the beauty in everything. I get bubbling energy in the body. If I have that feeling, I have tears in my eyes every time I hear the national anthem.*

> *The emotions are stirred. Yes, yes, I see deeper into things, seeing more fundamental aspects.*

4. ENHANCED INTUITION

Contact with the deepest mental levels often enhances intuition. Orienteering is a sport where the purpose is to run and navigate (using a map and compass) as fast as possible in a forest, passing through a number of checkpoints (controls) in a fixed sequence. Orienteering is thus a sport that is demanding both mentally and physically. Hanne Staff, a female orienteer who won four world championships and two World Cups, said that in many orienteering races she made decisions that appeared to be irrational at the time, but after the race, she realized that these choices enabled her to win. Thomas Alsgaard also emphasizes the significance of intuition—a quiet, deeper, more subtle mental level—for high performance:

> *You feel at once when there are things that are not as they should be, and you act based on intuition. Often it is just acting on gut feeling and instinct. … I have made very many choices without really knowing why, but I had a good feeling, and then in hindsight it becomes clear that it was just this little deviation, just this change that was needed to perform at the top. Many times I have made a crystal-clear plan about what I am going to do—a plan of my training program—but then I start to deviate from this plan without knowing why, and then it turns out that this deviation was exactly what was needed. (Laughter.)*

With respect to the world championship cross-country skiing relay in Val de Femme in 2003, Thomas tells the following story that further illustrates the significance of intuition:

> *The Swede Jörgen Brink cracked completely on the last leg. Everyone thinks that the race was settled on the hill just before the finish, where I passed him. But in reality the competition was determined long before this when I had a minute glimpse of Brink's face during one second at the top of a hill. I got some signals that something was about to happen. Brink was still running as fast as the rest of us, who were a considerable distance behind him, but there was something … just the one glimpse, during just the one second. I acted based on this signal. This was just the right time to do it. … I cannot explain why, and my team won.*

5. INCREASED INNER SILENCE

As we unfold the deepest levels of the mind, we become more restful and alert at the same time. One of our top-level managers reports on inner calmness during high performance: "As chairman of the board, I always participate on a 'meta-level,' e.g., observing the wholeness in a calm way, and then participating in the summing-up after the debate." Another top-level manager noted, "When sitting in meetings or during various other activities, I often get a feeling of being an observer to what is happening." A third manager explains, "I have experienced this in situations where the pressure has been large and where my outer calmness has been important for achieving results, preventing 'catastrophes.'" The professional opera singer Carsten Stabell relates his experience: "At optimal performance the mind is absolutely calm and in balance."

6. GREATER HAPPINESS

Happiness may be present at all levels of development, but it seems to reach new heights during post-conventional moments. Gjelsten talks about top performance using phrases indicating that it was an intrinsically satisfying experience:

> *Even if I placed badly, I was satisfied with the result. The performance was a positive experience: Lighter state of mind, no friction, happiness, intense euphoria, and exhilaration.*

The female soccer player Hege Riise—who was part of the Norwegian national team winning one gold medal in the Olympic Games, one world championship, and one European championship—recalls experiencing "bubbles" of happiness during top performance. Heidi Tjugum says with respect to her best performance, "The competition was just joy, plainly speaking." Trude Dybendahl Hartz—a cross-country skier who won one gold, three silver, and two bronze medals in world championships, and three silver medals in the Olympic Games—describes optimal performance as "I feel an enormous joy."

Our top-level managers frequently report happiness while resting with eyes closed. One manager said, "I often feel an extreme feeling of happiness. Energy flows in a current throughout the whole body—like several comfortable waves—like a mild wind." Another executive explained that it is "The experience that everything is right … an intense happiness and inner joy." A third recollected, "I have experienced complete happiness—just a great feeling of happiness."

Katharina Hager-Saltnes, a cellist in the Oslo Philharmonic Orchestra, describes her experience after optimal performances: "A feeling of having been successful, of having communicated something to the audience, gives much satisfaction afterwards. You feel you are successful as a musician and person. This is perhaps the prime mover of musicians!" A professional trumpet soloist talks about feeling happiness during his best performances:

> *During concerts, I often feel I am a natural part of the music. Without losing focus on myself, I feel I am part of something greater. This is always experienced as something positive, and creates a feeling of calmness and security. ... The feeling of happiness from playing is the greatest feeling I can describe in words.*

Flow—Another Special Performance Experience

Flow is triggered by a match between challenge and ability (Csíkszentmihályi, 1975; 1991). During flow, the performer feels good because there is a sense of mastery and there is no boredom since ability is stretched a little. Energized focus, full involvement, spontaneous joy, and success in the activity may naturally result. Frequency of flow experiences does not vary with age.

It is important to not confuse post-conventional experiences and peak experiences with flow. Compared to post-conventional experiences and peak experiences, flow is a more general experience. This experience may thus be reported by the full range of persons—from those who are limited to the most surface mental levels of action and senses to those who enjoy contact with the deepest mental levels of feelings, ego, and Transcendental Consciousness (see Table 1.1).

Jackson and Csíkszentmihályi (1999, p. 13) comment, "while an event that involves flow may also be defined as a peak experience or a peak performance, there are many other opportunities for flow that are not reserved for moments of highest happiness or best performance." This suggests that post-conventional and peak experiences may be in the "upper end" of flow.

Prior research correlates flow states with high performance in athletes and musicians. For example, O'Neill (1999) reported that high-achieving music students reported more flow experiences than moderate-achieving students did; and Jackson et al. (2001) found a correlation between flow and optimal performance in athletes.

Post-conventional Traits of Top Performers

> *The difference between the best and the second best lies in the head.*
> — Thomas Alsgaard, world-class cross-country skier

Recall that post-conventional traits depend on uncovering the feeling and ego levels. Below, we present a number of such traits that emerged from our research on the athletes, managers, and musicians: Self-reliance, growth-orientation, setting high goals, focus on excellence, powerful mind, intrinsic motivation, playfulness, learning while performing, and pro-action instead of reaction. The first two are from the content analysis of the interviews with the athletes (Boes et al., 2014).

1. SELF-RELIANCE

A powerful mind naturally translates into a high degree of self-reliance. Self-reliance was described by our high performers using words like self-responsibility, self-sufficiency, and self-referral. It was evident that many of the top athletes took full responsibility for their own life and performance—the coach, manager, team, or other advisors were secondary. Thomas Alsgaard says (Harung, 2012, p. 46):

> *Taking responsibility for one's own development. There is nobody else that can create a winner. No coach or manager that can create a winner. This is one of the things I learned from my father when I was 14, and that is self-sufficiency. Make your own plans and decisions, and evaluate yourself. In the final analysis there is no one else that can help me.*

Ingrid Kristiansen is a long-distance runner who set six world records from 5000m on track to marathon. Her marathon world record held for 13 years. She is the only runner in the world who held world records in 5000m, 10000m, half-marathon, and marathon at the same time. Ingrid states:

> *I have never been very preoccupied with what other people think. I have stood my grounds on the choices that I've made. I have never been afraid*

of what other people think about me and my performances. I have gone my own ways.

Self-reliance is closely related to self-referral. For a self-referring person, like Thomas Alsgaard, the inner reality is primary, and the outer—what other people say and what the environment tells you—is secondary. Sir Alex Ferguson, who for 26 years was the highly successful manager of Manchester United Football Club, writes in his autobiography (2013, p. 253):

A central component of the manager-player relationship is that you have to make them take responsibility for their own actions, their own mistakes, their performance level, and finally the result.

2. GROWTH-ORIENTATION

Growth-orientation, in our study, was marked by such words as improvement, progress, optimization, and priority of process. This sense of continuous improvement and growth energizes the top performers to excel beyond their own personal bests. For example, Bjørn Rune Gjelsten withdrew from the turmoil of celebrations and media 30 minutes after winning major races; he wanted to analyze and learn from the day's race while it was still fresh in his mind. Thomas Alsgaard also talks about his intense focus on learning that starts immediately following the finish of a race:

Then analyze. OK, I won today, but there were things that did not function. Half an hour after finishing with an Olympic gold medal, I am underway with the preparations for the next race—to eliminate all mistakes and become better. This is the reason why some people can win year after year.

Heidi Tjugum likes growth and finding new solutions:

It is fun to challenge myself. This is what keeps me motivated. I am the type that easily gets bored when things are too simple. Routine is OK, but I like some surprises. I like it when I have to think, have to find new solutions. I like it when I feel that OK this is a new problem and now I have found a new solution. Then I am very happy, even though the solution perhaps was not the optimal one.

Thomas Alsgaard says, "I require progress the whole time. When I am not making progress in a race, I instead use that competition to analyze, to try to find out what is wrong, so that I can amend it and make sure that I make progress in the next competition. I need progress all the time." The peak-performing female track runner Ingrid Kristiansen reflected:

> *What can I do to improve myself? ... My son would often ask me why I was training two times a day since I already was the world's best. I would reply that if you think you are the best, you are done. You always have to believe that there is something you can improve upon.*

3. SETTING HIGH GOALS

In order to reach excellence, you need to formulate high goals that you are deeply committed to. Goal setting will impact several of the other mental attributes related to top performance, such as growth-orientation, continuous learning, and pro-action. Goal formulation was described by two world-class athletes in the following terms:

> *You have to have a big goal, like far ahead, but it's the small goals that will keep you going and going, and finally you will reach that big goal ... take these small steps to a focused goal, and then you will reach this [bigger] goal (Tae Kwondo). I've made this goal very strong for me. I've made this commitment to myself. This is something I really, really, really want to do (Orienteering).*

4. FOCUS ON EXCELLENCE

The world-class orienteer Hanne Staff recollects an important race when she ran straight into 14 controls (checkpoints), but missed on the 15th. Afterwards she analyzed only those controls where her navigation had been successful. In contrast, her major competitors in hindsight put a lot of attention on controls they had missed. Hanne thinks this difference at least partly explains why she won several major races when her competitors appeared to be equally fit and able. The peak-performing handball goalkeeper Heidi Tjugum tells the story that once she had a rare bad day; afterwards she watched videos of only her very best matches!

In 1984, Charles A. Garfield, a psychologist at the University of California at San Francisco, wrote the now classic book on *Peak Performance: Mental Training Techniques of the World's Greatest Athletes*. He defines optimal performance in sports (p. 159):

> *A feeling of self-confidence, a positive attitude, or an inner sense of optimism about being able to perform well is reported as a key factor that determines whether the athlete can transform a potentially threatening athletic challenge into success while maintaining poise.*

5. POWERFUL MIND

We find that even in demanding endurance sports, the mind is very important for success. Jimmy Connors, an athlete known for his mental toughness, has often stated that professional tennis is 95 percent mental. Bjørnar Valstad, who won four world championships and one World Cup in the sport of orienteering (running and navigating using a map and compass in a forest), has experienced the power of the mind:

> *In the beginning [of your career] you don't think so much about the mental aspects. There are a lot of people training the same way ... physically. They have the same strength; everything is the same. But why is someone beating others? I don't think it is how they are doing their interval [training] sessions. I think it's very much about thinking the right way.*

Thomas Alsgaard echoes the importance of the mental game:

> *I train with someone who is equally good as I, equally strong physically, and who wins the training session during the summer. But when we come to the winter, the result is exactly as before [i.e., I win].*

Top performers use deeper, more powerful levels of the mind to improve their performance by affirmation and visualizing upcoming competitions. For a powerful mind it is especially important to focus on positive things, i.e., to put the attention on what one wants to achieve, and not on what one does not want to happen. Thomas Alsgaard recollects:

> *I would also like to think that the mental visualization, which takes place during the whole preparation process each season, is what differentiates the best from the second best. ... When I am at the starting line of an important competition—a world championship or an Olympic race—then I have already run this race a hundred times in my head, or at the back of my head. ... I have many more hours with technical training in bed than what I have out in the forest.*

Research shows that when we visualize we activate the same areas of the brain that are activated when performing the actual activity that is visualized (Pfurtscheller et al., 1997). This means that visualization has the potential to improve the actual performance.

6. INTRINSIC MOTIVATION

Recall that higher psychological development brings with it a shift from extrinsic motivation (winning, money, power, and fame) to intrinsic motivation (happiness, autonomy, mastery, and purpose). Thomas Alsgaard appears to be intrinsically motivated:

> *The main goal is to compete with myself—it is every day to make progress. The whole time. If I make progress every day, I know that the results during competition will be good. But the results are secondary in a way. The media need to focus on the gold medal, but in reality it is not this that matters to me. What matters to me is internal; it is very little commercial. … To put it acutely: I have won many races but been dissatisfied. On the other hand, I have been number 4 or 5 in a race while being very satisfied. It is my evaluation of the work I have done which is important.*

Several other world-class athletes also express that the process is primary, i.e., the fulfillment of performing is in itself more gratifying than winning the gold medal. The offshore boat racer Bjørn Rune Gjelsten says, "That special feeling is most important, not the trophy."

With respect to extrinsic motivation, surveys in USA, Germany, Russia, and India have found that those who consider money, career, and appearance to be most important are less satisfied with their life than those who emphasize good relations with other people, development of their talents, and doing something for society (Schmuck et al., 2000). In fact, strong ambition is often accompanied by anxiety and depression. The *War for Talent* study by McKinsey, a world-leading business consulting firm, found that "the best people are attracted to companies that fulfill the deep, personal need for meaning while making contributions to society—beyond the profit motive" (Aburdene, 2007, p. xxv).

Growing intrinsic motivation is illustrated by the public Norwegian power generation company Statkraft, a world leader in renewable energy (Evensen, 2009b). This company has reduced the waste from its headquarters canteen by 43 percent and the associates are served organic food in a green indoor environment throughout the year. Although primarily an arrangement to improve the well-being of its associates, these improvements have also had a positive influence on the motivation and quality of people applying for jobs. In particular for younger job seekers it appears to be important to work in a company that enacts social and environmental responsibility.

7. PLAYFULNESS

Playfulness is an attribute that is related to the search for happiness and meaning that we find in intrinsic motivation. Thomas Alsgaard notes:

> *It is a game. Sport is play. The day it becomes serious, then you are done. This is what differentiates the very best from the next best. The very best will to succeed; the next best must succeed, those that are desperate to succeed. [It is] important to keep it a game. It has to be fun. This is what it started with, and this is what it finished with. That it was great fun. The joy and that it was a lot of play.*

8. LEARNING WHILE PERFORMING

One way the peak performers achieve continuous improvement is through the ability to learn and perform at the same time. This learning while performing, available in higher psychological development (Torbert, 1991), is illustrated by Thomas Alsgaard:

> *Always evaluation. Continually. The whole time. Every day, every training session. Every minute is evaluated. ... [It] has to do with honesty. I have to dare facing reality and acknowledge that I have a problem, instead of believing that it will be solved by itself. ... It is spontaneous. I feel at once when there are things that are not as they should be. It may be minute details that show that things are moving in the wrong direction.*

The USA discus thrower Al Oerter won the Olympics a record four times. Charles Garfield (1984, p. 156) observed:

> *Maintaining the ideal performance state was not—at least for Oerter—a complicated process. He describes his own athletic poise as "the ability to step outside yourself" and to calmly ask how you can correct or improve your performance. ... He had a great ability to calmly self-criticize and self-correct. ... He did not struggle with his own ego to do this.*

9. PRO-ACTION INSTEAD OF REACTION

For those who enjoy post-conventional psychological development, a primary focus is on prevention and pro-action, while reaction and treatment (of a problem after it has occurred) usually dominate at earlier growth stages (Torbert, 1991). Thomas Alsgaard explains the benefit of pro-action and its connection to intuition:

> *Like in a race, in a finish duel, you just have to do something. I have to make a choice before my competitors realize that a choice must be made; I have to be in advance. I cannot wait to see what they do, and then I have to analyze it. This will simply take far too much time. ... Many things happen that I cannot explain why or what has happened—it is just that I have done it. Nine out of ten times it was the correct choice. ... I have to. Otherwise, I am left behind. I have to be ahead. When the senses are very open, I feel when there is something that is about to happen. And if I manage to act then, before the others do what they have been thinking about, I do something surprising, and that outmaneuvers them. I take the initiative.*

Theory of Psychological Development

The above eloquent temporary experiences and lasting attributes reflect the highest, post-conventional stages of psychological development. The full range of such development will now be discussed so that the reader can appreciate the significance of these experiences and attributes. Psychological development is found to follow a fixed sequence that parallels changes in brain development. During psychological development, lower stages are reconfigured to form a higher stage, which contains skills and capacities not found in earlier stages.

It is important to note that many skills—such as communication skills and study skills—within limits can be developed through practice. However, psychological development is more fundamental, requiring a fundamental reordering of how our brain works. Thus, such shifts cannot be consciously brought about by training or willpower.

Similar stages have been identified in cognitive, moral, and ego or self-development. We describe each of these streams of development and give examples of performance benefits resulting from such growth.

I. COGNITIVE DEVELOPMENT

The Swiss psychologist Jean Piaget's (1954, 1972) work provides the foundation on which theories of cognitive, moral, and ego or self-development have been based. The reality of an infant is governed by the most surface levels of behavior and senses related to the immediate surroundings—food, parents, toys, etc. During development, awareness progressively expands to include deeper, more abstract, and more powerful mental levels. For each step one differentiates from the current level and reintegrates at a deeper level, e.g., from identifying with thoughts to having thoughts. At any time, the deepest mental level enlivened is the main contributor to our developmental stage and our perspective on life.

Piaget described cognitive development in terms of four hierarchical stages that are unfolded in an invariant sequence across cultures over the first two decades of life, with each sequential stage including and extending earlier stages. Each new stage of development brings with it a broader construction of the way we consider ourselves, others, and the world, and the way we make meaning of experience and life. In this way, each consecutive stage provides the framework for higher levels of performance and quality of life.

The first two stages in Piaget's model are seen in young children. The third stage, *concrete operations*, typically develops between the ages of 7 to 11 years. Intellectual development in this stage is characterized by logical and systematic manipulation of symbols (e.g., algebra), which are related to concrete objects. Rules are considered absolute and must be followed. Today, over half of adults still function at the concrete operations level.

The last stage in Piaget's model is *formal operations*. In formal operations the person can see beyond the immediate experience and identify underlying principles and forces at work. They can think about multiple variables in systematic ways, can formulate hypotheses, and can think about abstract relationships and concepts. It is estimated that currently only 40 percent of adults are in this stage and then only in their chosen field or profession. Cognitive development tends to stop in early adulthood. For example, general intelligence is remarkably stable after the age of 20 (Smith and Smith, 2005).

Benefits of cognitive development on performance. Cognitive development influences skill development. The musicians we studied took part in two cognitive skill tests. First, the Stroop test measures reaction times when naming color words written in an ink different than the color word itself—such as the word "red" written in blue ink. When the font-color and word are different, they activate conflicting responses. The Stroop task yields the time to resolve competition between the fast automatic response of reading words (low road response in Figure 2.1) and the slow controlled response of attending to and naming the color (high road response) of the font the word is written in (Stroop, 1935). Compared to the average-performing controls, the professional musicians performed significantly faster on this test, which means that they were able to more readily resolve conflicting responses and keep on task.

The second test measured vigilance and speed of picking up rare unexpected tones and rare expected tones. Compared to the amateur musicians, the professional musicians picked up unexpected tones significantly faster, and there was a trend towards this difference for the expected tones. Faster processing means that the professional musicians processed more information per unit time.

Together, these two tasks show that the professional musicians took in more information and resolved conflicting points of view more quickly than the controls. These two cognitive skills have obvious application in business and sports. A company will prosper if it is the first to pick up new trends in the market or in technology. A soccer player would benefit from the ability to quickly change his or her next move based on the unexpected behavior of an opposing player.

Research shows that developing particular cognitive skills can benefit performance, e.g., general intelligence is predictive of higher performance (Robertson and Smith, 2001). Higher scores on creativity, response inhibition, and cognitive flexibility were found in Swedish elite soccer players as compared to low-division players (Vestberg et al., 2012). In fact, the top scorers in elite soccer placed amongst the top two percentages of the whole Swedish population on this measure.

2. MORAL DEVELOPMENT

Lawrence Kohlberg (quoted in Wilber, 2000, p. 45), a pioneer in moral development, recognized three major moral transitions: "The individual starts out amoral and egocentric ('whatever I want' is what is right), moves to socio-centric ('what the group, tribe, country wants' is right), to world-centric (what is fair for all people, regardless of race, color, and creed)." Higher moral development thus means considering a larger context for making ethical decisions—for instance the impact of actions on others, society, and environment, rather than merely on one's own individual needs. More advanced levels of moral reasoning emerge developmentally and are part of growth of psychological development in general. Typically, moral reasoning is stable during adulthood (Kohlberg, 1984).

Higher moral reasoning is associated with higher levels of cognitive development (Gibbs et al., 1990) and, in our research, with higher levels of brain integration. The study of the cognitive and brain mechanisms underlying ethical decision-making reveals that (1) ethical decision-making appears to be distinct from other types of decision-making processes, (2) ethical decision-making entails more than just conscious reasoning, and (3) emotion plays a critical role in ethical decision-making (Salvador and Folger, 2009). Ethical decision-making thus involves both rational (*reflective*) and emotional (*reflexive*) components. See also the two roads of brain functioning shown in Figure 2.1.

Benefits of moral development on performance. Moral behavior in business and industry has received increasing attention in recent years as is evident from numerous media disclosures. Surveys reveal that 80 percent of Americans do not trust corporate executives and—worse—that roughly half of all managers do not trust their own leaders (Hurley, 2006). There has also been much focus on moral development and sport due to considerable unethical behavior amongst athletes (Long et al., 2006), e.g., the numerous doping scandals in professional cycling.

Fortunately, there is research bringing out the benefits of acting morally. Measures of moral development have been found to be related to integrity and ethical professional performance (Arnold and Ponemon, 1991; Trevino and Nelson, 2007). A study interviewed 48 executives who had achieved great success by adhering to moral conviction, and found that "Morality is a positive force in human life, not just a set of stifling constraints" (Damon, 2004, p. 14). A meta-analysis of over 90 years of research has found that integrity (closely related to moral development) and general intelligence together give the best prediction, explaining 42 percent of performance levels (Robertson and Smith, 2001).

We studied moral reasoning by using a standardized questionnaire that asks people why they would, for instance, keep a promise or save another's life (Gibbs et al., 1990). We found that the top performers in management, music, and sports *all* scored significantly higher than their average-performing controls on moral reasoning. This finding is heartening because it suggests that honesty pays. Of course, the core benefit of acting morally is improved conscience, improved self-esteem, improved image, and a good reputation—but it also helps that performance is enhanced!

3. EGO OR SELF-DEVELOPMENT

Jane Loevinger (1976; Loevinger et al., 1985) is the pioneering researcher in ego or self-development. She found that each progressive stage of development brings with it a broader framework to make meaning of ourselves, others, and the world. Qualities of the higher stages include tolerance, coping with conflicting inner needs, cherishing of individuality, toleration of ambiguity, and broad scope. Assessments of psychological development in managers have noted the leadership styles characteristic of different developmental stages (Kuhnert and Lewis, 1987; Rooke and Torbert, 2005). Merron et al. (1987) correlated developmental stages, as measured by Loevinger's test, with performance on an in-basket exercise, a test used in hiring and promoting employees.

Ego or self-development is rare after the ages of 17–20 years, as reported in a quantitative review of more than 90 studies with over 12,300 subjects in a wide range of age groups (Cohn, 1998, p. 140). Not only does ego or self-development typically stop in early adulthood, but different individuals stop at different stages—even with similar education and socioeconomic background (Torbert, 1991).

Table 3.1 shows the typical distribution of ego or self-development in today's adult population (Cook-Greuter, 1999/2000). Pre-conventional development is an immature range—normally found in children—that corresponds to perceiving life in terms of behavior and the senses. It is estimated that 10 percent of adults are in this domain. Typically, the deepest mental level uncovered by the current adult population lies in the region of the thinking mind and the deciding intellect, i.e., in the conventional range, which is the reality of about 80 percent of adults. It is unfortunate that only about 10 percent of adults have reached the post-conventional range, which permits more complex thoughts plus an increasing refinement of feelings and ego. It is also unfortunate that as few as 1 percent of the adult population reaches ego-integration—the highest level of psychological development.

Table 3.1 Approximate Percentage of Today's Adult Population in the Three Ego-developmental Ranges

Ego-developmental Range	Deepest Mental Level Uncovered	Approximate Percentage of Today's Adult Population
Pre-conventional (normally found in children)	Action, senses, and desire	10%
Conventional	Concrete thinking and intellect	80%
Post-conventional	Feelings and ego	10% (at the upper end: Ego-integration or self-actualization: 1%)

From conventional to post-conventional development. To illustrate the extensive potential for performance improvement that exists today, let us contrast the personal characteristics and behavioral styles of conventional development with post-conventional development, as summarized in Table 3.2. The post-conventional reality includes and so can understand the conventional reality. A conventional person, however, is restricted to the conventional perspective. It is evident that the transition from the conventional to the post-conventional range spontaneously unfolds many of the success factors described in the performance literature.

Consider, for example, path-finding versus path-following. An *achiever* (upper end of conventional range) is limited to operating within a conventional frame and restricted to the implementation of an existing strategy. In contrast, post-conventional people have extensive freedom of thought, i.e., independent of conventional thinking, but they are not purposefully untraditional. Thus, a *strategist* (lower part of the post-conventional range) ceases to take the frame of the existing system for granted and becomes interested in what the best system would be. In other words, while the achiever may be able to cut a way through a jungle, the strategist climbs to the top of a tree to see if he or she is in the right jungle (Torbert, 1991). With more post-conventional people in society we can thus expect more innovation and progress in all fields of human activity.

Table 3.2 Contrasting Conventional with Post-conventional Individual Development

From Conventional Individual	=>	To Post-conventional Individual
Path-following	=>	Path-finding
Dependence	=>	Greater autonomy and self-reliance
Mistrust	=>	Greater trust
Control	=>	Collaboration
Win-lose interpersonal strategies	=>	Win-win interpersonal strategies
Narrow craft perspective	=>	Greater wholeness
Exclusive of others	=>	Inclusive of others
Stereotyped thinking and attitudes	=>	More open, reflective, tolerant; moderated attitudes
Reactive and treatment	=>	Proactive and preventive
Short-term perspective	=>	Long-term perspective
Ambivalence to feedback	=>	Embracing feedback
Externalizing blame	=>	Taking responsibility for own life
Ethics based on following others or norms	=>	Sound ethics, internalizing what is right and wrong
Deficiency-orientation	=>	Growth-orientation
Focus on problem solution	=>	Focus on process and problem finding (e.g., new business opportunities)
Focus on immediate problems	=>	Comprehensive strategy
Efficiency—doing things right	=>	Effectiveness—doing right things
Drawn to what is urgent	=>	Focus on what is important
Smothering conflict	=>	Airing conflict
Conflicts are common and often difficult to resolve	=>	Fewer conflicts and creative problem-solving
Socially derived self-identity	=>	Internally derived self-identity
Extrinsic motivation: Beating others, and gaining money, fame, and power	=>	Intrinsic motivation: Happiness, autonomy, mastery, and purpose

Ego-integration. Beyond the strategist is ego-integration, which lies at the upper end of the post-conventional range. Ego-integration corresponds to the fullest unfolding of individual ego. Ego-integrated individuals display healthy and productive values and attitudes. They naturally behave in ways that reflect integrity, greatly increased creativity, and refined human values such as righteousness, justice, and beauty. They display an enhanced capacity to make meaning of experience, to perform consciously, and to handle complexity, and are said to enjoy frequent peak experiences and good luck or fortunate coincidences (Maslow, 1968). Birgitta J. Halbakken, a viola player in the Oslo Philharmonic Orchestra, reported on the experience of luck: "It can be that people I want to be in contact with show up or the situation just gets right for a meeting without any involvement from my part."

Benefits of ego-development on performance. An investigation of 497 managers in different industries showed that 80 percent of senior managers were at the post-conventional range compared to only 10 percent at this level in the general population (Rooke and Torbert, 2005). Their research also suggested that only those managers in the post-conventional range showed the consistent capacity to innovate and to successfully transform their organizations.

We found that the excellent athletes scored significantly higher on ego or self-development than the average-performing control athletes. Recall that the top athletes referred to the post-conventional themes of self-reliance, growth-orientation, and wholeness significantly more frequently than the controls (Boes et al., 2014). The interview brought out the importance of both mental and physical development for high-level achievement in sports.

Overview of Some Benefits of Higher Psychological Development

Higher psychological development spontaneously results in increasingly more comprehensive repertoires for effective performance, as is illustrated by the following examples:

- Enhanced self-identity, delight in paradoxes and anomalies, understanding that all frames through which the world is seen are relative, understanding the uniqueness of each individual and situation.

- Increased holistic and intuitive grasp of the situation, transcending of personal style, airing rather than smothering conflict, managing interpersonal tension in positive ways, tolerance of ambiguity, and excellence.

- Improved ability to handle cognitive complexity (i.e., simultaneous differentiation and integration), more moderated attitudes, openness to disconfirming information and adjustment in thinking, more effective discernments of the intents and strategies of others, better interrelationship of decisions, and more appropriate strategy development.

Need for a New Approach

The management and performance literature describes desirable high performance attributes, thinking, and behavior. For example, Stephen Covey (1989) outlines habits of highly effective people, such as be proactive; think win-win; seek first to understand, then to be understood; and sharpen the saw (principles of balanced self-renewal). Geoff Colvin (2010), senior editor at large at *Fortune* magazine, writes that world-class performance depends on attributes like intrinsic motivation, intense focus and concentration, and endurance (long-term perspective). When asked by the newspaper *Aftenposten* why she at the age of 33 became the most-winning female Winter Olympics athlete, the cross-country skier Marit Bjørgen said, "It is because I have been patient."

The *theory* is absolutely correct—if these attributes and ways of thinking and behaving could be adopted, performance would certainly be raised to substantially higher levels. However, the critical question is *how* to develop these desirable qualities in *practical life*. Admittedly, some of the features are skills that—within limits—can be developed by practice and learning, e.g., think win-win or seek first to understand. However, what is often overlooked is that *all* these multiple features are various spontaneous expressions of the *single* factor of mind-brain development. Your current level of mind-brain development determines how you react to the world. This in turn reinforces that habitual response. Only by breaking out of this vicious cycle—by actively facilitating higher mind-brain development—can you significantly change your view of the world and so begin to *live* the desirable attributes. Otherwise, these features will unfortunately remain impractical ideals.

It seems that the public is increasingly becoming aware of the shortcomings of the more or less elusive literature in psychology, management, etc. that claims a "quick-fix" to high performance through consciously changing one's thinking, attitudes, and/or behavior. The lack of satisfaction here may in part explain why there is an accelerating interest in enhanced brain functioning as the basis of improved quality of life and performance—people want to deal with something that is concrete and real.

A shift to higher mind-brain development cannot be achieved by practicing more or harder—it can only be achieved by practicing "smarter." Chapter 7 outlines practical procedures for mind-brain development that enhance both individual and organizational performance.

Summarizing this Chapter

We have seen in this chapter that higher psychological development progressively transforms the way we perceive ourselves, others, and the world. This shift is towards more holistic, long-term, win-win, and proactive thinking and behavior. Such a growth spontaneously unfolds our potential for effective thought and action so that we can achieve temporary high performance within narrow domains. However, generalized and sustained world-class performance seems to belong only to unfolding Transcendental Consciousness, which will be discussed in the next chapter. Fortunately, it appears that uncovering Transcendental Consciousness to a large extent is independent of stage of psychological development, suggesting that ego-transcendence can be experienced and unfolded even while psychological development is still taking place.

Chapter 4

Third Performance Dimension: Lasting Peak Experiences—Gateway to Lasting Excellence

How do corporations achieve the challenging but lucrative goal of continuous innovation? The short answer, the only answer, is through the genius inherent in human consciousness.

— *Patricia Aburdene, American writer (2007, p. xvi)*

Peak Experiences—the Key to World-class Performance

The audience was listening closely when the first author of this book gave a presentation on peak experiences at the World Productivity Congress in Istanbul, 1995. In particular, there was one person who lighted up more and more as the talk progressed. As soon as the lecture finished, this person came up to me and gave me a big hug, and thanked me very much. Why? Peter Bild explained that he had had many peak experiences in his life, but nobody had ever explained to him what they meant. Hence, he was grateful for understanding what such moments are—especially that they represent something highly positive. Perhaps you also have had such highly rewarding moments without appreciating their full significance?

Abraham Maslow observed that two of his teachers were different; they had a different orientation to and understanding of life. He went on to study over 100 people who were visibly successful and whom he considered to be self-actualized (see Chapter 3). Some of his subjects were historical and some contemporary. They included Abraham Lincoln, Thomas Jefferson, Albert Einstein, Eleanor Roosevelt, William James, Albert Schweitzer, and Benedict Spinoza. Maslow found that these people typically reported frequent peak experiences—short glimpses of transcendence characterized by great joy, beauty, wholeness, aliveness, perfection, completion, justice, order, effortlessness, playfulness, and self-sufficiency. Maslow observes the significance of peak experiences (1968, pp. 80–81):

> *The peak experiences of pure delight are for my subjects among the ultimate goals of living and the ultimate validations and justifications for it. ... The peak experience is only good and desirable, and is never experienced as evil or undesirable. The experience is intrinsically valid, perfect, complete, and needs nothing else.*

Peak performers in a wide range of professions and activities report peak moments: Athletes such as Pelé (soccer), Billie Jean King (tennis), Thomas Alsgaard (cross-country skiing), and Sebastian Coe (running); poets such as Emily Brontë, Walt Whitman, and William Wordsworth; scientists such as Einstein, Maxwell, and Schrödinger; composers such as Beethoven and Mozart; and national leaders such as Vaclav Havel (Czech Republic) and Anwar el-Sadat (Egypt) have all reported a comprehensive range of such gratifying glimpses (Pearson, 2013).

WHAT TRIGGERS PEAK EXPERIENCES?

Peak experiences are often triggered by especially rewarding circumstances: (1) gratifying moments such as deep meditation or relaxation, prayer, harmonizing music, beautiful art, scenic nature, warm relationships, and weddings, (2) moments of high intensity such as during exams or when performing surgery, or (3) events following long anticipation and preparation, such as important competitions, exhibitions, or concerts. However, peaks may also occur during any ordinary activity.

These moments of highest happiness—which may be experienced as ineffable, beyond words—are sometimes seen as turning points in life, e.g., spontaneous remissions of disease or major changes in one's values and priorities.

Selection of Peak Experiences in World-class Performers

The following citations from our study of peak performers exemplify a selection of important qualities within seven groups of peak experiences: Greatly expanded awareness, everything is right, effortless action, automation in action, restful alertness, improved time management, and frequent luck and good fortune.

1. GREATLY EXPANDED AWARENESS

To succeed in a symphony orchestra, each player must integrate his or her own playing with the instructions of the conductor and the playing of all the other musicians. Previously, we talked about the importance of sharp focus or the tunnel for high performance. When experiencing "the tunnel," the performer is able to focus only on factors relevant to his or her performance and thus exclude all irrelevant input and thoughts. Such focus belongs to higher psychological development.

In contrast, a peak experience is characterized by the ability to combine sharp focus with a greatly expanded awareness that takes in the whole picture. The cellist Bjørn Solum in the Oslo Philharmonic Orchestra talks about the combination of sharp focus and expanded awareness during optimal performance: "experience myself as very tolerant and open at the same time as I am set on the target and have very high focus on the result." The soloist soprano Eli Kristin Hanssveen in the Norwegian Opera explains it this way: "During peak conditions it is nothing or almost nothing that can disturb the performance, even if I register everything that is happening." Billie Jean King, one of history's greatest tennis players, articulates a greatly expanded awareness—one that encompasses a place of total peace and calm and the audience (King and Chapin, 1974, p. 191 and pp. 197–201):

> *On my very best days I have this fantastic ... feeling of invincibility. ... I appreciate what my opponent is doing, but in a very detached, abstract way, like an observer in the next room. ... When I'm in that kind of state ... I feel that tennis is an art form that's capable of moving both the players and the audience. ... When I'm performing at my absolute best, I think that some of the euphoria that I feel must be transmitted to the audience. ... [I]t almost seems as though I'm able to transport myself beyond the turmoil on the court to some place of total peace and calm. ... It's a perfect combination of [intense] action taking place in an atmosphere of total tranquility. ... And when it happens I want to stop the match and grab the microphone and shout, "That's what it's all about." Because it is. It's not the big prize I'm going to win at the end of the match or anything else. It's just having done something that's totally pure and having experienced the perfect emotion.*

2. EVERYTHING IS RIGHT

The cross-country skier Trude Dybendahl Hartz indicates that she is enjoying a peak experience when she describes her best performances:

> *Enormous presence in yourself. More than a mental state—emotional and spiritual. Feel an enormous joy. Prepared. Alert. Balance between being settled and dynamic. Everything is right—as it should be. No analyzing—it only is. Witness to self. Strange experience. Extremely light version of myself. Almost as if I do not touch the ground.*

During peaks, the changing outer experiences come and go on the ground of a non-changing inner silent level of wakefulness, as is indicated by the words "witness to self" in the above quote. Witnessing in this context does not mean active cognitive processing or watching; rather it denotes the coexistence of inner, silent Transcendental Consciousness along with the activity of feeling, planning, thinking, sensing, and behaving. Outer behavior continues, but now it takes place on an expanded inner basis that supports but is not touched by this outer activity.

In contrast, Trude's worst competitions are characterized by "No particular joy. Much more attention on the world outside. Focus on all the excuses and explanations for why this is not going so well." During optimal performance while enjoying a peak experience, Trude appears to be fully in charge. But in her worst competitions she is worrying, and is focused externally and finding reasons for not performing at the top, a situation which reflects the conventional domain.

"Short-lived" and "pleasant," even "ecstatic," were adjectives our subjects used to express peak moments. One top performer reported a feeling of perfection. With no conscious effort they are in total control of the situation with no fears of failure.

Kenneth Ravizza (1977) at California State University at Fullerton was one of the first sports psychologists to describe how athletes felt during their greatest moments. He interviewed athletes of both genders and in 12 different sports—at levels ranging from recreational to Olympic—asking about their "greatest moments." A skier revealed, "Everything was so perfect, everything so right … there seemed to be tracks in the snow that my skis were made to fit in." The orienteer Bjørnar Valstad in our research also describes a peak moment in terms of everything being as it should be:

> *It's a very strong feeling when you're in the race and you know that this is how it should be. And you know that I'm not going to lose it. It's going to stay this way the whole race. ... When you're running some other competitions, sometimes when you don't get this feeling so strong, then suddenly you do something foolish, stupid, and you lose time. But during those really, really good competitions you can't get out of it. (Laughter.) On those days you have 100 percent control over your mind, but it's very relaxing—no stress at all.*

3. EFFORTLESS ACTION

We have previously noted that all physical processes follow the law of least action. Optimal performance during peaks is frequently described using words like least action, effortless, no resistance, and deep relaxation amidst dynamic activity, thereby reflecting action in accordance with the law of least action. Charles Garfield (1984, p. 95) writes about *sweet spots* or peaks:

> *... everything just seemed to flow automatically ... it was all very effortless. ... The feelings of glory or transcendence that athletes report derive from their ability to attain a high level of efficiency in their physical movements, a level of performance that requires complete harmony and cooperation between body and mind.*

Spontaneous right action is illustrated by Magnus Carlsen, who at the age of 22 was the highest-ranking chess player in history. In 2013, he won the regular World Chess Championship and in 2014 the World Rapid and Blitz Chess Championship. Carlsen says that it is important to create harmony between the chess pieces. When he plays well, he gets a strong feeling of harmony—that everything fits together so well. The goal is to get the good moves to come flowing by themselves (Madsen, 2013).

Trude Dybendahl Hartz describes her 10 best races using words like "No resistance. Living in an internal world. Absorbed. I am ready. Enormous presence. I act based on impulse." The handball goalkeeper Heidi Tjugum talks about automatic action: "Get that good feeling ... then it goes by itself. It is as if the body functions without me having to do something about it." Fredrik Fors, a clarinet player in the Oslo Philharmonic Orchestra, recalls effortlessness during peak performances:

> *During a concert, when everything works well and I have total control over the situation, ironically I feel that I can let go of the control and*

> *just go with the flow. It's a kind of feeling of happiness that makes my profession so wonderful. It is important for me to have total technical control and overview in order to allow myself to let go!*

The British track runner Sebastian Coe at one time held four world records: 800m, 1000m, 1500m, and 1 mile. Describing a race in 1979, when he set a new world record of 1:42.4 for the 800m, Sebastian is indicating effortless action (Coe and Miller, 1981, p. 66):

> *I had no particular sensation of speed and I think I could have run even faster, I wasn't exhausted at all at the end. It was a strange feeling—like being on autopilot ... and it just felt beautiful. But I would have been as happy on the night had I run 1:43.3 as I was with 1:42.4.*

Similarly, when breaking the 1 mile world record in 1979, Sebastian recollects that he was feeling very comfortable. The lack of effort was apparent even to the audience, as *US Track and Field News* reported: "What stunned most observers was his almost complete lack of fatigue after the race. No stumbling, no heavy breathing" (Coe and Miller, 1981, p. 74). In contrast, the finish when Coe won the 1500m at the 1980 Olympic Games in Moscow was fundamentally different (p. 142):

> *The mental agony of knowing that I had hit my limit. I tried to drive again at 40 meters out, and in the next few strides I knew I had nothing left if anyone came back at me. The anxiety over the last 20 meters was unbearable, and it showed on my face as I crossed the line. After a few yards, I sank down on my knees.*

It thus seems that a high level of performance is possible without having a peak experience. Through extensive training in a sport, a person acting in the domain of psychological development may achieve high performance (see Chapter 6). However, we propose that action during a peak experience is qualitatively different. It (1) is intrinsically more gratifying, (2) causes less wear and tear on body and mind, and (3) promotes generalized top performance in more complex areas of activity, at even higher levels, and on a sustainable basis. Similarly, Charles Garfield (1984, p. 160) talks about peak performance:

> *When an athlete is hitting the internal sweet spots—when timing is right and the motion is smooth—the skills levels are higher, the athletic motions quicker, more forceful, more accurate. ... The athlete is performing "within" himself or herself, under control, within the limits*

to motion beyond which human tissue is overstressed. And there is one more advantage to this smooth-running vision of athletics: Endurance.

4. AUTOMATION IN ACTION

Bjørnar Valstad recollects that when he won the 2004 orienteering world championship classical distance he enjoyed automation in action:

> *I feel quite safe in some way. … And all the things I'm doing are in some way just sitting in the background. Mentally, in orienteering we have map-reading, but it's going automatic. … When I'm in this mode, there are no negative thoughts. It's like sitting in a car with an autopilot and just sitting watching. I notice something happen in front of me and I need to do something and then back again, and you just sit there. When [in] the race, this is quite simple. It's getting to know how to practice this, which is most difficult.*

If this special experience were a cognitive act, it could have been brought about consciously. However, this was clearly a spontaneous experience. Automation in action is reflected by Bjørnar's expression that map-reading or navigation is "going automatic." In another part of the interview, he told us that it was as if he was running a marked route (route marked with ribbons), while orienteering in reality involves hundreds of decisions using a map and a compass to successfully navigate through a race normally having many checkpoints and often lasting 1–2 hours. "No negative thoughts" and "this is quite simple" show that Bjørnar experienced inner happiness and ease of functioning.

Other writers have also noted that high performance may be related to automation: "It's like everything goes automatically without [your] thinking" (Jackson and Csíkszentmihályi, 1999, p. 75). The female handball player Susann Goksør Bjerkrheim was part of the Norwegian national women's handball team that won one gold, one silver, and one bronze in world championships, two silver and one bronze in Olympic Games, and one silver and one bronze in European championships. Susann reported automation in action when her team won the world championship in 1999:

> *When I have this extreme alertness, the body reacts automatically. I am freed from thinking how to move the body—everything goes by itself. Instantaneous coordination of mind and body, body spontaneously reacts to what you observe. It goes by intuition. There are two steps. First, read the situation and make right choices. There is a high*

> *adaptability and critical choices are made correctly. Second, the body moves effortlessly—there is perfection in mind-body coordination. It is a great relief when everything goes by itself. No effort. Easy. Unbelievable self-satisfaction. Nothing is difficult. A kick. A high.*

5. RESTFUL ALERTNESS

A professional first violin player explains how during optimal performance she felt an inner silence coexisting with dynamic activity, thus giving expression to a state of restful alertness during a peak experience:

> *When I won the audition for Oslo Philharmonic Orchestra, I was focused, silent inside, at the same time as I tried to perform at my very best. The focus felt as a great silence, but not calm, on the contrary an active super-concentrated silence necessary for the activity to be at its very best. I knew that without this silence, I would lose focus and thus my chance to win.*

Hans Morten Stensland, a musician in the Oslo Philharmonic Orchestra, says this about his optimal performances:

> *Particularly when I perform concerts, but also during practice, I experience that I can observe what is happening from the sideline. … During the performance I often experience a particularly intense concentration and alertness; I comprehend absolutely every detail; it is in a way like everything around me is happening in slow motion in such a way that I have more time to orientate myself. Difficult passages become easier to play. Besides, I often experience that the mode of expression in the music is more evident for me and that I can play around and vary in a different way than usual. I feel that I am mastering the situation and that I have lots of mental surplus. At the same time, I am totally calm. I feel without limitations.*

6. IMPROVED TIME MANAGEMENT

Deeper mental levels are associated with changed perception of time and improved time management. Bjørn Rune Gjelsten experienced this during his best boat races: "The perception of time changes. … Captures almost everything. Picks up much more nuances than normally." The female soccer player Hege Riise talks about optimal performance using words like "A slow motion feeling where I know I will succeed." The handball player Susann Goksør Bjerkrheim describes a European Cup match when she was playing for Bækkelagets Sports Club in Oslo:

> *When three seconds were left, we needed one more goal to win. There was a free throw and I got the ball. In less than one second, I first had to evaluate the position and movement of all the other five players in my team. I decided that none of them were in a good position to score. Then I decided to shoot myself even though I was not in a very good position. Next, I made the necessary moves, and was able to score. I experienced an extreme wakefulness. I absorbed and processed an unbelievable amount of information in an unbelievably short time.*

7. FREQUENT LUCK AND GOOD FORTUNE

To succeed, a manager may rely more on intuition or hunches in making decisions, and profit from good luck. We found a trend for more luck in the top-level managers compared to low-level managers. Another study concluded that the higher the manager is in the organization, the more likely he or she is to perceive luck as affecting outcome (Parnell and Dent, 2009).

In his book *The Outliers*, Malcolm Gladwell (2009) emphasizes the importance of luck for individual success. He gives examples of how several of the most successful software programmers—like Bill Gates—all were born around 1955 when the timing was perfect for making successful breakthroughs in computers. Gladwell continues that lucky breaks don't seem like the exception with software billionaires and rock bands and star athletes. They seem like the rule. A female player in the Oslo Philharmonic Orchestra relates luck to a powerful mind:

> *When I have expressed within myself a strong determination to achieve something, e.g., happiness and well-being, I have experienced that things have "turned out all right" in the most incredible ways. Often this is related to an inner decision, which then apparently "is sorting things out" and the stronger the desire, which means the stronger the decision is, the more favorably I experience the way it turns out right.*

Luck spontaneously unfolds with higher mind-brain development. Thomas Alsgaard points out that it is usually the same persons who have luck all the time. He himself has won more than half of his gold medals in Olympic Games or world championships in the endurance sport of cross-country skiing with less than a one-second margin. The soccer player Hege Riise indicates that frequent good fortune was part of her success:

> *I always am where the ball falls down. The right place at the right time. A pass comes that I 'know' will fall down on my foot—and I shoot a volley and score.*

One of our top-level managers says, "It happens all the time that I am surprised at how things fall into place." Another comments, "I have many times had the feeling of being in the right place at the right time." A third CEO writes:

> *It seems to me that I often have luck in business, when buying a property or something. It often turns out that those business options that did not come through would not have been so smart. However, I would have chosen these businesses options if something outside my control had not come in the way.*

Explaining luck. How can we explain luck or good fortune? We see luck as a feature that increasingly unfolds with higher mind-brain development, which involves more and more contact with the deepest mental levels. Transcendental Consciousness—the source of thought—is of particular importance here. Later in this book, we propose that the experience of Transcendental Consciousness is also the direct experience of the *unified field of natural law,* which modern quantum physics has glimpsed as the source of the universe. Luck and fortunate coincidences could thus result from our ability to think and act while established in the source of natural law so that we gain its support (Maharishi, 1986). A female violin player in the Norwegian Opera reported:

> *I still relate to it as a stroke of good luck that exactly all of my desires became fulfilled when I auditioned for the opera orchestra in 2003. It went just perfect. That it was just the day that I—even though I was a bit late and was supposed to play almost at the beginning (so I did not feel totally warmed up when I went in)—got such a flow that I could perform at my best in exactly that short moment (but I had of course also practiced). … Perhaps I believe that you can guide yourself in the direction you desire, and make it right if you so desire and work for it. I think that I've had very much luck in my life. Much has been good, and not-so-good things have evolved in the right direction.*

Luck is therefore much more fundamental than strategy, communication, problem-solving, or financial management. However, luck does not replace traditional training and education in any profession—on the contrary, they complement each other in our quest for peak performance.

A second important factor explaining luck is the support of the social context. If there is a need for a new product or service, then the environment will support its development. This is explored in Chapter 5.

8. SENSE OF INVINCIBILITY

Features like effortlessness, no resistance, automation in action, and luck may contribute to the feeling of invincibility often reported during optimal performance. Susann Goksør Bjerkrheim talked about the power of a coherent team: "I feel invincible when this community mood is there." The world-class cross-country skier Thomas Alsgaard recollects:

> *When everything is at the very highest level, then I feel invincible. The uphills are not long enough nor steep enough. Extremely good sensation.*

Handball goalkeeper Heidi Tjugum describes a sense of being invincible when she says:

> *OK, this I master so well that it is just for the opposing players to come at me. Just shoot! Whatever you do, you will not be able to score.*

Feeling unbeatable is related to no fear, another aspect of a peak experience. The British golfer Tony Jacklin recalls a peak experience during a tournament (Leonard, 1974, p. 42):

> *It's not like playing golf in a dream or anything like that. Quite the opposite. When I'm in this state everything is pure, vividly clear. I'm in a cocoon of concentration. And if I can put myself into that cocoon, I'm invincible.*

Recall that Pelé also uses the word *invincible* to describe his very best performance. The professional American baseball player Tony Gwynn says, "It's something way beyond confidence. I mean, I'm usually fairly confident, but this is like ... I don't even know what the word would be" (Kreidler, 1989).

Our Research on Peak Experiences in World-class Performers

All four world-class studies assessed the frequency of peak experiences reported by top performers, as compared to average-performing controls, using the *Survey of Peak Experiences*. This paper-and-pencil test is adapted from a survey to assess higher consciousness (see later) and consists of four questions: Three that reflect ego-transcendence and one on luck (Cranson et al., 1991):

1. *Transcendental experiences during relaxation with eyes closed*: "During practice of relaxation, meditation, prayer, or any other technique—or when you have relaxed or had a quiet moment—have you then experienced a completely peaceful state, a state when the mind is very awake, but quiet, a state when consciousness seems to be expanded beyond the limitations of thought, beyond the limitations of time and space?"

2. *Transcendental experiences during waking activity*: "Have you experienced that while performing activity there was an even state of silence within you, underlying and coexisting with activity, yet untouched by activity? This could be experienced as detached witnessing even while acting with intense focus."

3. *Transcendental experiences during sleep*: "During deep sleep, have you ever experienced a quiet, peaceful, inner wakefulness? You woke up fresh and rested, but with a sense that you had maintained a continuity of silent self-awareness during sleep?"

4. *Luck or fortunate coincidences*: "Have you experienced that your desires are fulfilled in a way that seems to be caused by coincidence or luck? You may have experienced that the circumstances arrange themselves to fulfill your desires without your direct action."

For each question, the subject indicated frequency of the experience—ranging from "never to my knowledge" (0) to "all the time" (11). We also asked the subjects to write down sample descriptions of such glimpses, using their own words. These descriptions are used by the scorer to evaluate whether the experiences are genuine or not.

FREQUENCY OF PEAK EXPERIENCES FROM THE SURVEY

Using questions 1–3 (excluding luck), we found the following frequencies of performers' reporting at least one peak experience in their life:

- Athletes: 73 percent of the world-class athletes and 71 percent of the controls.
- Managers: 91 percent of the top-level managers and 82 percent of the controls.
- Musicians: 100 percent of the professional musicians and 80 percent of the controls.

The average frequency for the three studies across all subjects was 84 percent. Maslow (1971) observed that practically everyone has peak experiences, but not everyone knows it. An interview study of a random sample of 1,000 persons in the San Francisco Bay area concluded that virtually everyone appears to have peak moments of one kind or another in their life (Wuthnow, 1978). The conclusion is therefore that peaks are completely natural and generally available. Seeing the prevalence of such elevated experiences and their association with successful performance, it is important to bring them to the attention of people in general.

While most of our subjects reported at least one instance of peak experiences, a closer examination of the data reveals interesting differences between the peak performers and controls:

1. *Performers within several professions.* The top performers in this pilot study had significantly more frequent experiences compared to controls on Question 1 (Transcendental experiences during relaxation) and Question 3 (Transcendental experiences during sleep).
2. *Athletes.* There were no significant differences in the frequency of peak experiences between the two groups of athletes.
3. *Managers.* The top-level managers reported significantly more frequent peak experiences during relaxation (Question 1) and a trend for greater luck (Question 4).

4. *Classical musicians.* The professional musicians had significantly more frequent peak experiences on Questions 1, 2, and 3, i.e., during relaxation, activity, and sleep. Abraham Maslow observed that classical music readily triggers peak experiences.

Why did the high-performing musicians in our study report more peak experiences compared to their controls than the managers and athletes? A possible explanation is that music includes functioning at levels deeper than feelings. When performing, musicians focus on sound emerging from silence, on perceiving and bringing about refinement of the most delicate impulses of sound—in a sense "hearing" these sounds emerge from and submerge into silence. In addition, harmonizing music stimulates the level of feelings, which is closer to Transcendental Consciousness than the intellect (the primary domain of management) and the body and senses (the primary domain of sports).

PEAK EXPERIENCES AND AGE

The frequency of peaks seems to remain stable after early adulthood:

- On the third question of the Survey of Peak Experiences, which asks for experiences during sleep, it was found that students did not improve over time (Cranson et al., 1991).
- Students are reported to have at least as frequent momentary transcendental experiences as older subjects (Wulff, 1991).
- The frequency of peak experiences in a group of artists and musicians did not correlate with age (Panzarella, 1980).
- In our investigation of peak performers and controls (N=142), age explained only 1.4 percent of variation in reported frequency of peak experiences during waking activity.
- Age also does not affect the frequency of flow experiences (see Chapter 3).

PLATEAU EXPERIENCES

Abraham Maslow (1971) writes that the effect of the transient peak experiences—which often contain an element of surprise or even disbelief—inevitably remains with the person, and may over time result in more lasting plateau experiences. While the plateau experiences are characterized by much the same qualities as the peaks, the plateaus have a more serene and calm nature since the person is now more familiar with transcendence. Maslow (1968, p. 106) noted that activity during both peak and plateau experiences spontaneously translate into peak performance:

> *What takes effort, straining, and struggling at other times is now done without any sense of striving, of working or laboring, but "comes of itself." He is no longer wasting effort fighting and resisting himself, muscles are no longer resisting muscles. … Such a person is seen as possessing a stability or calm steadiness … as if they know exactly what they are doing, and were doing it wholeheartedly, without doubts. … The great athletes, artists, creators, leaders, and executives exhibit this quality of behavior when they are functioning at their best.*

Although Maslow (1971, p. 270) had deep insights into the farther reaches of human nature, he admits that "it is unfortunate that I can no longer be theoretically neat at this level." That the Western theoretical model of higher development is incomplete is also noted by Csíkszentmihályi with respect to flow (which includes peak experiences): "The experience of flow is still one of the least understood phenomena in sport" (Jackson and Csíkszentmihályi, 1999, back cover).

NEED FOR AN EXPANDED MODEL

Most Western psychologists consider ego-integration—as described in Chapter 3—to represent the apex of human development. However, ego-integration does not bring in the most fundamental mental level, transcendence, which is present during peak and plateau experiences. While Maslow and a few other Western thinkers have written about peak experiences, modern psychology does not offer an integrated theoretical framework to explain these glimpses. To find a satisfactory understanding of top performance we therefore need to move outside Western social science, and instead turn to the age-old traditions of the East.

Higher Consciousness in the Vedic Tradition of India

> *Established in Yoga [Transcendental Consciousness], O winner of wealth, perform actions.*
>
> — Bhagavad Gita, ancient Vedic text
> (Maharishi, 1969, p. 135)

In contrast to the West, thinkers in the East—such as the Vedic and Chinese traditions—have deeply explored higher human development. We will focus on the Vedic tradition of India since we have found it to be most comprehensive in theory and most effective in facilitating human development in practice. Maharishi (1986, 1997) has placed the knowledge from the Vedic tradition in the framework of modern Western science. This is known as *Maharishi Vedic Science*.

Maharishi Vedic Science outlines seven states of consciousness (Alexander et al., 1990), as shown in Table 4.1. The first three are the common states of sleep, dreaming, and waking consciousness. The ranges of psychological development described in Chapter 3 are sub-states within waking consciousness. The fourth state is Transcendental Consciousness, which is pure self-awareness without content. The alternation of Transcendental Consciousness with waking develops over time the next three higher states, which are permanent: Cosmic (unbounded) Consciousness, Refined Cosmic Consciousness, and Unity Consciousness.

Table 4.1 Seven States of Consciousness

State of Consciousness	Sense of Self	Awareness of Object
1. Sleep	No	No
2. Dreaming	No	Illusory
3. Waking	Lower self	Yes, but only more surface aspects
4. Transcendental	Higher Self	No
5. Cosmic	Higher Self	Yes, but only more surface aspects
6. Refined Cosmic	Higher Self	Yes, surface and subtlest aspects of object
7. Unity	Higher Self	Yes, objects are appreciated as the dynamism in the wholeness of the Self

We can now view Maslow's peak and plateau experiences in the framework of Maharishi Vedic Science. Peak experiences appear to be momentary glimpses of any of the four higher states of consciousness and plateau experiences appear to be longer periods of the three highest states of consciousness.

Since Western science until now has been almost exclusively concerned with psychological development, the tendency is to put higher consciousness as a continuum after pre-conventional, conventional, and post-conventional—a so-called "fourth tier" (Cook-Greuter, 2000). However, we suggest that psychological development and growth of higher states of consciousness are *parallel dimensions* of development. Higher states of consciousness do not require full psychological development as a prerequisite for their growth. Thus, higher states can be reached even before psychological development is completed. While parallel dimensions, they do seem to interact.

The transitions to each of the four higher states of consciousness are much more far-reaching than the transitions between the pre-conventional, conventional, and post-conventional ranges in psychological development. Table 4.2 contrasts qualities of post-conventional growth with those of higher consciousness.

Table 4.2 Contrasting Post-conventional Development with Higher Consciousness

Post-conventional Individual	Individual in Higher Consciousness
Temporary peak experiences	Permanent higher consciousness
Considerable happiness	Permanent bliss
Temporary world-class performance	Continuous world-class performance
Peak performance in narrow domains	Generalized peak performance
World-class performance for relatively simple tasks	World-class performance for both simple and complex tasks
Do less and accomplish more	Do least and accomplish most
Wide awareness	Unbounded awareness
Less bound by time and space	Transcends time and space
Greater comprehension	Feeling a union with others, nature, and the world
Self-sufficiency	Sense of invincibility
Considerable luck and good fortune	Life supported by natural law
Intrinsic motivation (happiness, autonomy, mastery, and purpose)	Action satisfies the need of the time, i.e., timely action
Consciousness mainly aware of objects (object-referral)	Consciousness aware of both itself (self-referral) and objects
Sound ethics, internalizing what is right and wrong	Compassion for all life
Actualizes individual potential	Actualizes nature's potential

The Vedic tradition sees higher consciousness as the birthright of every individual. With growth in higher consciousness, the person would be less governed by outer circumstances and more governed by inner values, feelings, and thinking. Mind-brain development involves a shift from object-referral to self-referral. Recall the 1,000,000,000,000,000 connections between brain cells. The vast majority of these connections—over 90 percent—are *internal* connections among the neurons, with less than 10 percent of the connections devoted to sensory processing (Raichele, 2010). These 90 percent bring out the capacity of the brain for a rich spectrum of inner experiences and growth.

Four Higher States of Consciousness

We will now illustrate the inner nature of the four higher states of consciousness by quotes that bring out key attributes of such experiences.

THE FOURTH STATE—TRANSCENDENTAL CONSCIOUSNESS

Transcendental Consciousness is the most fundamental level of human awareness—a state of restful alertness, inner wakefulness, and unbounded awareness. In Transcendental Consciousness, the mind is completely silent, but fully awake, and free of thinking, feeling, and perception. This is the simplest form of human awareness or the ground state of consciousness, which underlies all thoughts, feelings, and actions. Maharishi (1986, p. 25) defines Transcendental Consciousness as follows:

> *When consciousness is flowing out into the field of thoughts and activity, it identifies itself with many things, and this is how experience takes place. Consciousness coming back onto itself gains an integrated state, because consciousness in itself is completely integrated. This is pure consciousness, or Transcendental Consciousness. From this basic level of life emerge all fields of existence, all kinds of intelligence.*

The following experience from our research suggests a glimpse of Transcendental Consciousness by the world-class handball goalkeeper Heidi Tjugum:

> *I have quite a lot of times experienced a state where I am completely inside myself and everything else disappears. This is a form of relaxation. ... And there is nothing that can touch me. It feels very good. It is not that those periods are so very long. But it is beautiful to have them, once a week or once a day.*

Transcendental Consciousness seems to be associated with a joyful experience, as is reflected in "It feels very good" in the above quote, and in many of the other citations we present. In one study, 68 percent reported the experience of Transcendental Consciousness in terms of the absence of time, space, and body sense, the framework that gives meaning to waking experience (Travis and Pearson, 2000).

Physiology of Transcendental Consciousness. The physiological state during Transcendental Consciousness can be characterized as *restful alertness*. It is different from sleep (rest alone) and different from focused attention (alertness alone). Instead, restful alertness during Transcendental Meditation (TM; Maharishi, [1963] 2001, 1969) is associated with the *coexistence* of restfulness and alertness. Indices of restfulness include decreased breath rate, decreased skin conductance levels, and decreased blood flow to subcortical brain areas responsible for arousal (Dillbeck and Orme-Johnson, 1987; Ludwig, 2011). Simultaneously, increased alertness of the mind is suggested by increased blood flow to the prefrontal cortex and increased alpha1 (8–10 Hz) brain waves (Travis et al., 2010; Ludwig, 2011). Alpha1 EEG is a reliable brain marker of restful alertness. It is seen whenever the attention is turned within but is undirected. It is seen when one is imagining a story compared to speaking it out. It is seen just before the "aha" moment and indicates being wide awake—alert consciousness that is the source of all creative solutions and high performance.

Alpha1 waves are a marker of the background screen of conscious awareness on which everyday thinking occurs. Gamma (30–50 Hz) and other faster frequencies are responsible for computing the details of the specific thought processes. When one transcends, the gamma activity decreases, corresponding to the quieting of thinking, and alpha activity remains, corresponding to the maintenance of the screen of awareness by itself in Transcendental Consciousness (Travis et al., 2010).

THE FIFTH STATE—COSMIC CONSCIOUSNESS

By alternating the experience of Transcendental Consciousness with activity the subjective experience and corresponding brain functioning of Transcendental Consciousness begin to be integrated into daily life. Like a flower gradually opening up, life becomes more in terms of inner fullness and less in terms of outer activity. Over time, the human nervous system becomes so refined that the inner silent experience of Transcendental Consciousness coexists on an ongoing basis with the changing states of waking, dreaming, and sleeping—this is called Cosmic Consciousness. The human mind now maintains two opposite modes of functioning simultaneously: Silence and dynamism, wholeness and point, Transcendental Consciousness and activity. This state of coexistence of opposites is sometimes called *witnessing*. Witnessing is not a verb—one can't practice witnessing—it is a noun. Maharishi (1969, pp. 98–99) explains:

> *The activity assumed by an ignorant man to belong to himself—to the subjective personality that he calls himself—does not belong to his real Self, for this, in its essential nature, is beyond activity. The Self, in its real nature, is only the silent witness of everything.*

When we maintain the stable experience of Transcendental Consciousness during everyday activity, the individual no longer is inhibited by stress and lack of fulfillment. During optimal performance, the handball goalkeeper Heidi Tjugum talks about an advanced experience where she just is a witness to what is happening:

> *Sometimes I have felt that I am an observer—I just watch what happens. This is a good feeling; it is a very beautiful feeling, it is not that I feel I don't have control. But it goes by itself—in reality I do not have to initiate anything at all. Extremely here and now—nothing else matters. And it is unbelievably good. Beautiful experience. These feelings are unbelievably nice. They stimulate me to taking on further challenges. Obviously, this is what I am longing for every time I go to a training session.*

Thomas Alsgaard also indicates a glimpse of witnessing during activity: "In a way you become a spectator." Recall the top-performing orienteer Bjørnar Valstad talking about a peak experience when he won a world championship:

> *Mentally, in orienteering, we have map-reading, but it's going automatically. ... It's like sitting in a car with an auto-pilot and just sitting watching. I notice something happen in front of me and I need to do something and then back again, and you just sit there.*

Physiology of Cosmic Consciousness. Brain patterns in subjects reporting Cosmic Consciousness have been investigated—both during sleep and waking:

1. The experience of a continuum of inner awareness during sleep is the principal subjective indicator of the state of Cosmic Consciousness. The brain waves were measured during sleep on long-term practitioners of Transcendental Meditation (Chapter 7) who reported the experience of inner wakefulness during sleep.

The measurements showed alpha1 (wakefulness) along with delta (deep sleep) waves (Mason et al., 1997).

2. Brain patterns during waking have also been investigated in individuals reporting the state of Cosmic Consciousness. Long-term TM practitioners reporting the experience of Cosmic Consciousness exhibited higher scores on the Brain Integration Scale during challenging computer tasks (Travis et al., 2002). Higher levels of brain integration thus characterize both successful people and individuals in Cosmic Consciousness. A second study investigated the subjective and psychological picture of individuals reporting Cosmic Consciousness. The individuals in Cosmic Consciousness exhibited a more self-referral orientation to life, and they had higher levels of emotional stability, openness to experience, moral reasoning, and vigilance—and higher brain integration (Travis et al., 2004).

THE SIXTH STATE—REFINED COSMIC CONSCIOUSNESS

So far development has been in terms of *inner* transformation where our conscious awareness is expanded to fathom deeper and deeper mental levels—ultimately uncovering Transcendental Consciousness, the higher Self. This is Cosmic Consciousness. Yet, in the *outer* world, we still see things as we did before—seeing only the surface levels of objects. From Cosmic Consciousness, further development is through gradual refinement of perception of the outer world. We appreciate finer levels of an object—this appreciation is increasingly less in terms of differences and increasingly more in terms of harmony. This refinement is the development of Refined Cosmic Consciousness, as illustrated by the following quote (Alexander and Boyer, 1989):

> *Generally, whenever I put my attention on an object (for example, when looking at scenery out the window, or sitting in the kitchen), I become aware of the subtler qualities of the objects around me. For instance, when looking at a tree, I first become aware of the object as it is—a concrete form bound in space and time. But then I perceive finer aspects of the object coexisting along with its concrete expression. On this subtler level, objects are perceived as almost transparent structures of soft, satiny light (unlike harsher, normal daylight) through which the very essence of life appears to flow. This flowing field of life underlies and permeates the objects of perception. Perceiving these finer aspects of creation completely nourishes the finest aspects of my own being.*

The role of the heart in higher development. The growth to Refined Cosmic Consciousness is propelled by culturing the feeling level through putting one's attention on what unites rather than separates in relationships, such as harmony, love, service, and happiness. Today, the focus in education and society is on the thinking mind and the deciding intellect, the cognitive level (Chapter 1). This has created substantial progress, mainly in engineering and technology, but the enlivenment of deeper levels is needed to create a high quality of life and widespread excellence. It does not seem that one needs to be an intellectual to reach higher consciousness, which is primarily an experiential reality.

The significance of enlivening the feeling level is brought out by a story in the ancient Vedic literature. Shankara was a teacher who had four students. Three of the students were highly learned and intellectual and spent the day debating sophisticated intellectual questions. In contrast, the fourth student Trotakacharya served his teacher and fellow students with food, laundry, etc., i.e., he was primarily exercising the heart value. The story goes that it was Trotakacharya who was the first student to reach higher consciousness.

THE SEVENTH STATE—UNITY CONSCIOUSNESS

> *I know well that there is a state in which we experience undivided unity.*
> — Martin Buber, Austrian scholar and philosopher

Unity Consciousness is the highest level of human development in which everything—inner and outer—is experienced in terms of the Self. Differences are still there—otherwise life and activity would not be possible—but the experience of wholeness and harmony predominates, and differences are secondary. Maharishi (1969, p. 307) explains that in Unity Consciousness "the Self, which held Its identity as separate from all activity in the state of Cosmic Consciousness, finds everything in Itself."

This highest state is characterized by a greatly expanded awareness that encompasses the performance, the audience, the environment, and ultimately the universe as a whole. A 42-year-old male piano soloist in the Oslo Philharmonic Orchestra in a poetic way expressed the coexistence of sharp focus and a greatly expanded awareness during a peak:

> *It is difficult to describe, but it feels like experiencing a kind of eternity, contrary to everyday life, which is in continuous movement.*

The 52-year-old professional viola player Birgitta J. Halbakken recollects:

> *As if my inner expands to include the activity of the whole orchestra and even the audience. … A quivering pleasurable sensation at the same time as a total focus is on the activity. The mind doesn't just listen, but is a part of the music, which together with space, audience, co-players, and conductor become a wholeness.*

A similar experience was described by a skier: "I was really blending into the snow, the mountains. … I wasn't different from the hill. The whole mountain was part of me" (Ravizza, 1977). The world-class basketball player Bill Russell from the Boston Celtics echoes such experiences in terms of a shared reality that "would surround not only me and the other Celtics, but also the players on the other team, and even the referees" (Russell and Branch, 1979, p. 155).

CONSCIOUSNESS AS A FIELD AND INDIVIDUAL CONSCIOUSNESS

Can we understand this experience of union with others and the environment from the perspective of modern science? Let us consider what modern physics has to say about the structure of matter. Similar to the mental levels (Table 1.1), there are layers in the physical world. From the gross to the subtle these layers are visible matter, molecules, atoms, elementary particles, and four fundamental fields—gravity, electromagnetism, the weak force, and the strong force. A field is a non-local pervasive wholeness that underlies and influences the objects within its range, i.e., the gravitational field in an unseen way keeps the moon rotating around the earth, and the earth around the sun. Beyond these four fields, physics now glimpses the *unified field*, which extends throughout the universe and lies at the basis of everything physical within it: Matter, forces, time, space, and the natural laws that are functioning in time and space (Yau and Nadis, 2010). So far the unified field of physics is only a conceptual reality and many competing theories attempt to define this underlying unity. While still debated, these models better describe observable interactions than any previous theories in physics.

The quantum physicist John Hagelin (1987, 2012) argues that the unified field glimpsed by physics is identical to pure consciousness—which we contact during Transcendental Consciousness when our mind settles down completely. In other words, that mind and matter are fundamentally united. A similar point of view is expressed by several other leading physicists. Sir Arthur Eddington (1974, p. 276), a renowned British physicist, concluded,

"The stuff of the world is mind-stuff." The German physicist Max Planck, who first discovered the quantized nature of the subatomic world, stated, "I regard consciousness as primary. I regard matter as a derivative of consciousness" (quoted in Klein, 1984). The American physicist and Nobel laureate Eugene Wigner (1970) wrote, "The next revolution in physics will occur when the properties of mind will be included in the equations of quantum physics."

In both India and China there are long traditions that view nature as fundamentally unified. This underlying unity has been expressed in the Upanishads of the Vedic literature that discuss the nature of the Self: "The microcosm and the macrocosm are one. ... That which is smaller than the smallest is bigger than the biggest. ... That which is far away is within" (Pearson, 2008).

Emergence of individual consciousness. Western science has regarded human consciousness as emerging from brain functioning. However, William James (1963; see also Travis, 2012b), the founder of psychology as an academic discipline in America, argued that none of the empirical findings of science about the brain contradict the notion that the brain may serve to reflect or transmit a transcendental, infinite continuity of consciousness underlying the phenomenal world, rather than produce consciousness anew.

Similarly, the ancient Vedic texts suggest that individual consciousness is the *reflection*—through the agency of the brain—of the non-local, pervasive field of consciousness. The more refined the brain is, the more of the field of consciousness is expressed in individual consciousness. Consider an analogy where the sun's rays are reflected by a glass of green water. Then the reflection is only green. By gradually purifying the water, the quality of the reflection will become purer and brighter until it gains the same quality as the sun when the water is 100 percent pure (Maharishi, [1963] 2001). Similarly, with the growth of higher consciousness in the individual, the brain is gradually refined so that it is able to reflect more and more of the underlying field of consciousness.

Contrasting Psychological Development with Higher Consciousness

Psychological development is the growth of specific individual attributes and abilities. Higher consciousness is the transformation to what it means to be fully human.

During psychological development the lower self grows, including mind, intellect, and feelings. This reflects individual differences in genetically programmed tendencies as well as education and life experience. Psychological growth is realizing individual potential and results in a progressive unfolding of the ability to temporarily perform at a high level in one or a few narrow domains, e.g., success in management or teaching.

Growth of higher consciousness, on the other hand, is not constrained by specific individual genetic and epigenetic endowment, but is a *universally* available developmental potential. Realizing the Self provides the basis for achieving sustained and generalized peak performance in a wide range of activities.

These two developmental dimensions to a large extent unfold independently of each other. This means that higher consciousness may be available *before* one has reached, for instance, the post-conventional range. A study of a group of people reporting stabilized higher consciousness found that only 27 percent of them were measured to be in the post-conventional range of ego or self-development (Travis and Brown, 2009). Although this is about three times the current norm of 10 percent, it nevertheless indicates that full psychological development may not be a prerequisite for higher consciousness. Other researchers have found that persons in a wide range of psychological development enjoy peak experiences (Maslow, 1968; Panzarella, 1980), and this is also evident from our own research on world-class performers and their controls.

If full psychological development is not a prerequisite for the transition to higher consciousness, then higher consciousness is generally available and so excellence may be closer at hand than commonly thought. Since the two dimensions interact, psychological development probably continues after there has been a transition to higher consciousness.

Summarizing this Chapter

This chapter has provided an outline of higher states of consciousness, the apex of human development. We cited many inspiring peak experiences during optimal performance from our studies of world-class performers. To get a comprehensive model of this advanced dimension of human growth, we turned to higher consciousness as outlined in the ancient Vedic tradition of India, and revived today by Maharishi. The Vedic model provided a framework for understanding how an individual can attain sustainable peak performance in a wide range of activities.

Today, only about 1 percent of adults have reached ego-integration, the highest stage of development in Western psychology. In addition, most people enjoy brief peak moments only once or a few times during life. Fortunately, since psychological development and higher consciousness to a considerable extent are two parallel dimensions, higher consciousness may be available before reaching the summit of psychological development. This is good news, since it shows that there is an extensive potential for mind-brain development and performance improvement in the general population. Thus, sustainable world-class performance in higher consciousness is closer than was initially thought. The next chapter will continue our description of the foundation of excellent performance by outlining the benefits for individual performance of higher development of the organization and society in which the performer operates.

Chapter 5

Fourth Performance Dimension: Higher Organizational and Societal Development—Getting to Shared Excellence

> *... an assembly is significant in unity; united are their minds while full of desires.*
>
> *— Rig Veda, 10.191.2–4, ancient text from India*

We have previously seen the power of individual peak experiences in creating individual world-class performance. Similarly, a collective or shared peak experience may express itself in superior collective performance, as the following quote from basketball suggests. Bill Russell was the key player on the most successful basketball team ever, the Boston Celtics, who won 11 USA championships in 13 years. Bill described playing in a collective peak experience as follows (Russell and Branch, 1979, pp. 155–158):

> *Every so often a Celtics game would heat up so that it became more than a physical or even mental game, and would be magical. ... When it happened, I could feel my play rise to a new level. It came rarely, and would last anywhere from five minutes to a whole quarter, or more. ... It would surround not only me and the other Celtics, but also the players on the other team, and even the referees.*
>
> *At that special level, all sorts of odd things happened: The game would be in the white heat of competition, and yet somehow I wouldn't feel competitive, which is a miracle in itself. ... The game would move so quickly that every fake, cut, and pass would be surprising, and yet nothing could surprise me. It was almost as if we were playing in slow motion. ... There have been many times in my career when I felt moved or joyful, but these were the moments when I had chills pulsing up and down my spine. ... On the five or ten occasions when the game ended*

> *at that special level, I literally did not care who had won. If we lost, I'd still be as free and high as a sky hawk.*

Notice how Bill Russell is speaking about experiencing a shared reality among everyone on the court—him and his teammates, the players on the other team, and even the referees. This shared reality has been termed *collective consciousness* (Maharishi, 1976b, 1995).

Collective Consciousness

> *Just as the consciousness of an individual determines the quality of his thought and behavior, so also there exists another type of consciousness for a society as a whole; a* collective *consciousness for each family, city, state, or nation, having its own reality and the possibility of growth. The quality of the collective consciousness of a society is a direct and sensitive reflection of the level of consciousness of its individual members.*
>
> — Maharishi (1976a, p. 2)

Previous chapters have examined dimensions of development of mind and brain, also called development of individual consciousness. We have seen that the individual stage of development is a good predictor of the individual's level of performance and accomplishment. However, to fully understand individual performance, we must also include the influence of the stage of development or quality of the social context in which the performer operates (see Figure 1.1). *Collective consciousness* is a term that covers any collection of individuals. Each individual is embedded in several units of collective consciousness. Proceeding from the smallest to the largest, these units are family, team(s), department(s), organization(s), city, nation, and the world. The present chapter considers the effect of collective consciousness, this most expansive, fourth performance dimension, on individual and collective performance. The level of collective consciousness of any unit is primarily a function of the quality of the individuals that make it up:

$$\text{Level of collective consciousness} \approx f(\text{mind-brain development of all members}) \quad (5.1)$$

The quality of integrated functioning of the billions of cells in our body, including the brain, determines the stage of individual mind-brain development. Similarly, the level of consciousness of *all* the individuals in a group determines the level of collective consciousness of that group. Our *Unified Theory of Collective*

Performance states that higher collective consciousness provides the basis of higher collective performance in any industry, field of activity, or society.

For each unit of collective consciousness there is a reciprocal relation between the stages of individual mind-brain development and the stage of growth of collective consciousness. The different units of collective consciousness will also have a reciprocal effect on each other. For instance, the collective consciousness of an organization is affected by the mind-brain development of its members as well as by the contributions of the city, nation, and world collective consciousness.

NATURE OF COLLECTIVE CONSCIOUSNESS

> *I can feel a great love towards those I'm playing together with. It feels like you are united on both an intellectual and an emotional level. I feel happiness about the situation and a quiet contentment together with a worked-up joy about how great it is to play, and to master what I have been practicing.*
>
> — Ida Bryhn, viola player in the Oslo Philharmonic Orchestra, talking about optimal performance

How can we explain the tight reciprocal relation between the members of a collective consciousness? It was suggested in Chapter 4 that consciousness is a field, i.e., similar to gravity or the electromagnetic field. When you talk on your mobile phone, this is unseen communication through the electromagnetic field. Similarly, we are influencing others and being influenced by them through the unseen, underlying field of collective consciousness.

Greater integration or coherence within a unit of collective consciousness means greater complementarity among diverse individuals and groups, while greater incoherence is reflected in narrower perspectives, increased conflicts, and likelihood of social problems. Since the effect is reciprocal, if the collective consciousness is low, the influence on each individual member is negative, tending to reduce the level of happiness, performance, and accomplishment. Conversely, if the collective consciousness is high, this will spontaneously support harmony, peace, creativity, and progress for all members. Several writers point in the direction that organizations and society are fields of consciousness:

- Early psychologists such as Carl Jung conceived of a "collective unconscious" as a reservoir of experience of our species, the storage of humanity's collective experience common to everyone, which guides the development of the individual mind (Campbell, 1949).

- Peter Senge (1994, pp. 242 and 44), a MIT-based and internationally acknowledged pioneer within organizational learning, notes, "Most of the assumptions we hold were acquired from the pool of culturally acceptable assumptions," and, as a result, "we just find ourselves feeling compelled to act in certain ways." This high degree of consistency in shared attitudes, values, and ways of thinking, speech, and behavior—which defines an organizational culture—could reflect the underlying field of consciousness within that organization.

- In the book *Built to Last*, Collins and Porras (2002) discuss how a surprisingly strong organizational alignment is achieved in high-performing organizations—even in large multinational corporations, across diverse societal cultures, and over large physical distances.

- Margaret Wheatley (1994, p. 53) writes in her book *Leadership and the New Science*, "The longer I have thought about it, the more I am willing to believe that there are literal fields in organizations."

More generally, surface communication—through meetings, memos, emails, blogs, phone calls, kickoffs, etc.—in itself cannot fully explain the all-pervasive nature of a unit of collective consciousness. A complementary, more fundamental mechanism of communication exists if consciousness is a field—a communication which may be pervasive and instantaneous.

COLLECTIVE PERFORMANCE

> *[Best performance] will usually be in a concert where everything gets right. There is usually a large audience in the hall. It is actually necessary to have an audience in order for it to happen. ... An incredible feeling of happiness. You also have a very strong feeling of alertness. Almost like intoxication. ... You feel the body is working like it has never done before, and that you can accomplish anything. ... You become very aware of your co-players, and feel you have better than usual contact with them. You also feel to a very large degree that the audience is present, and that they receive everything you can give. It is actually the presence of the audience that triggers both the best and the worst performances.*
>
> — Gonzalo Moreno, pianist, Oslo Philharmonic Orchestra

Each unit of collective consciousness has its own level of functional identity. The quality of this wholeness not only impacts individual performance but also is the prime factor in determining the quality of overall collective performance. The level of development of the organizational consciousness expresses itself in the quality of its pervasive culture. Organizational culture in turn shapes hiring decisions and work expectations, and thus the quality of performance (Harung, 1999).

A study by the Korn/Ferry Institute (Zes and Landis, 2013) supports the idea that collective consciousness governs collective performance. This study searched 6,977 self-assessments from professionals at 486 publicly traded companies to identify the "blind spots" in individuals' leadership characteristics. A blind spot was defined as a skill that an associate counted among his strengths when coworkers cited that same skill as one of his weaknesses. The study also considered self-awareness—knowledge of one's strengths and weaknesses, ability to admit mistakes, and tendency to reflect, which all are attributes that spontaneously unfold with higher psychological development. To determine ROR (rate of return) for the shareholders, stock performance of the companies was tracked over 30 months, from July 2010 through January 2013. The study found that

1. Poorly performing companies' associates had 20 percent more blind spots than those working in financially strong companies.

2. Poorly performing companies' associates were 79 percent more likely to have low overall self-awareness than those in firms with robust ROR.

There is a tendency for people with a similar level of mind-brain development to group together in an organization, i.e., "birds of a feather flock together." This may be because people want to work with others that they can relate to and thus spontaneously seek organizations where the members have a similar worldview to theirs. The high-performing business G. C. Rieber in Norway recently carried out a survey of the values of their associates and found a high agreement with the company's values. Thus, the relationship between a new member and the organization seems to be binary: Either there is a fit and the new member will tend to stay for a long time; or there is a misfit and the new member usually leave the organization before long (Collins and Porras, 2002). Consequently, the level of organizational consciousness, culture, and performance tends to remain stable over long periods.

We have seen in previous chapters that it is rare for individuals to have significant mind-brain development during adulthood. Hence, this fundamental quality does not tend to change after we start work. Without interventions to enhance the development of the individual, it is difficult to fundamentally improve an organizational consciousness and culture. Therefore, it is advisable to start a new company by gathering a core of people with high mind-brain development.

LEADERS AS A REFLECTION OF COLLECTIVE CONSCIOUSNESS—A NEW CONCEPT

> *Government is the pure and innocent mirror of the nation, faithfully reflecting whatever is presented to it. ... Every decision of government is the expression of national [collective] consciousness.*
>
> – Maharishi (1995, p. 61)

If collective consciousness is the prime mover of an organization or a society, what is the impact of the leader? He or she will contribute to collective consciousness. However, since the leader is only one person, the larger the unit of collective consciousness, the less will his or her contribution be. Today, the leader is often credited with the success or failure of his or her organization. However, if collective consciousness determines collective performance and success, then it follows that the leader is a reflection of the collective consciousness he or she is leading (Harung, 1999; Harung et al., 1999). This reciprocal relationship suggests that a group of people gets the leader it deserves, and that the leader can only accomplish what the followers as a group allow and deserve. This reciprocity applies to any leader-led relationship: Public administration, business management, an orchestra, a coach or manager of a sports team, teachers, and parents.

Some business writers back the idea that the leader is a reflection of his or her organization. The leadership expert Warren Blank (1995) calls the currently popular idea that leadership power resides within a single person a mistake. In *Megatrends 2010*, Patricia Aburdene (2007) notes that the CEO is important, but just a piece of a much larger puzzle, and the fundamentals of the company are far more important than the CEO. A study considering the relationship between the coach and the team's level of performance in the Norwegian premier soccer league concluded (Natland, 2008):

1. Although the coach is considered to be very important for the team's achievements, there is no scientific support of this idea.

2. Firing the coach gives a small short-term performance benefit, but over time there is almost nil effect.

Similar findings have been made in England and USA. Replacing the coach does not significantly change the team's collective consciousness, and this explains why the performance level remains much the same afterwards. Firing the coach is costly. Thus, the common practice of blaming the coach when the team is not performing well is an expensive "scapegoat" procedure that does not address the underlying cause.

BALANCING TWO OPPOSING FORCES

Our research suggests that leaders have higher mind-brain development than their average associate (see also Torbert, 1991). How can this be reconciled with the theory that the leader reflects collective consciousness? The higher leader development comes about as a balance of two opposing forces:

1. Higher mind-brain development makes a better leader. We may call this application of our more general theory a *Unified Theory of Leadership* (Harung et al., 1995).

2. But the members need a leader that they can relate to and that thus reflects the level of collective consciousness they together form. Thus, due to opposing forces, the leader tends to have a moderately higher stage of development than the collective consciousness.

Let us elaborate on this point. The leaders' higher mind-brain development gives them a vision to lead their organization or society. However, even though the leaders may have a genuine desire to implement their progressive plans, without a wide enough perspective associates and citizens cannot support their leaders' intentions and actions. This may explain why politicians, who are elected based on platforms designed to fundamentally improve society, often fall short of achieving their inspiring goals.

As the collective consciousness rises in organizations and society, both the level of consciousness of the leader and of the organization will rise. Then we would expect a shift from a focus on the single boss to an emphasis on *all* associates and the collective consciousness they together form. This shift will lead to more and more equality of compensation, status, and influence of *all* associates. Collective wisdom will increasingly lead the company or society, and the leaders will see themselves as catalysts for improvement rather than as bosses who need to command and control others.

Model of Stages of Collective Consciousness

Individual mind-brain development takes place in discrete stages, as discussed in Chapters 3 and 4. Since each unit of collective consciousness is a collection of individuals, it follows that collective consciousness also should have discrete stages of growth. We use individual development as a template for understanding stages of collective consciousness. As individual *psychological* development has three ranges—pre-conventional, conventional, and post-conventional—so there should be similar ranges for collective consciousness. However, since only 10 percent of adults are at the *pre*-conventional range of psychological development, very few organizations function at that level. In any case, these organizations are not worth considering since they represent very low collective performance. Therefore, we will only consider organizations at the conventional and post-conventional ranges of psychological development. The conventional organizations are divided into two sub-ranges: Lower and upper. Moreover, as individual development includes *higher states of consciousness,* so development of collective consciousness should include functioning at levels beyond post-conventional: What we may call higher states of collective consciousness. On this basis, we describe four stages of collective development. Each stage is named after what matters most at that stage: Task, process, value, and consciousness (Harung, 1999).

The driver of growth in collective consciousness is the individual members uncovering progressively deeper mental levels in their own consciousness. Interventions that increase mind-brain development of the associates will thus contribute to higher stages of collective consciousness. We discuss this in Chapter 7.

Stage 1. Task-based: Lower Conventional Collective Consciousness

> *Worldly wisdom teaches that it is better for reputation to fail conventionally than to succeed unconventionally.*
>
> — John Maynard Keynes (2011), renowned British economist

The lower sub-range of conventional collective consciousness, which is very common today, emphasizes isolated tasks ("what") together with concrete and isolated measures and goals of performance, especially money, but also for example productivity. The core idea is often that "if you make money, then everything is OK." To satisfy the quest for money, it may even be acceptable to pollute the environment or underpay employees. Other factors that dominate are position, fame, and power, thus indicating that extrinsic motivation is common amongst associates.

The lower sub-range of conventional organizations is often characterized by authority centralized in a few top positions, top-down command-and-control, excessive bureaucracy, many and elaborate rules, focus on short-term goals (e.g., the next quarter's profits), information restricted to a few top positions, and training and privileges centralized at the top. The shared attitudes and human values of these organizations are often restricted or even negative: Fear-based performance systems; competing with others, not with oneself; unclear or limited purpose and goals; resistance to feedback and change; focus on satisfying superiors and not customers and society. Such organizations often have low levels of happiness, a shortage of meaningful work, and considerable struggle.

Stage 2. Process-based: Upper Conventional Collective Consciousness

As the collective consciousness rises, organizations in the upper part of the conventional range are defined by higher performance. Integrated processes ("how") may receive higher priority than isolated tasks. There may be more respect for individual differences and contributions, including team formation and self-management, decentralized participation in decision-processes and performance improvement, and more openness to feedback. These organizations are characterized by investment in raising the level of competence throughout the organization, inspiration, and reaching long-term goals. There is sharing of information and focus on satisfying the customer. A flatter, network-based organization is likely, but not required. There tends to be more joy and less struggle than in stage 1.

Stage 3. Value-based: Post-conventional Collective Consciousness

Post-conventional organizations represent a higher collective consciousness than conventional organizations. Table 5.1 contrasts selected properties of these two levels of collective development. The text that now follows will elaborate on and exemplify many of these differences. Since only about 10 percent of adults in today's society are post-conventional (see Chapter 3), there are some organizations approaching this relatively advanced stage, but very few that are fully at this stage.

Table 5.1 Contrasting Conventional with Post-conventional Organizations

From Conventional Organizations	=>	To Post-conventional Organizations
Command-and-control	=>	Collaborative
Boss-centered culture	=>	Shared ownership culture
Centralized	=>	Decentralized, self-management
Focus on CEO	=>	Focus on organization
Money primary	=>	People and meaning primary, value-driven
Punished for doing wrong	=>	Recognized for doing right
Fragmented	=>	Alignment
Survival of the fittest	=>	Co-evolution (beyond Darwin)
Focus on negativity and conflicts	=>	Focus on solutions and harmony
Mediocre performance widespread	=>	High performance the norm
Profit and non-profit organizations are distinct	=>	Both profit and non-profit organizations contribute equally to the quality of life of society
Performance aimed at satisfying narrow self-interests	=>	Simultaneous satisfaction of individual and collective needs
Money, technology, and energy as primary resources	=>	People, knowledge, and ideas as primary resources
Inequality	=>	Equality
Alienation, fear	=>	Integration, contribution, joy
Limitations, control	=>	Creativity, possibilities
Analytical, logical, rational	=>	Rational and intuitive, ethical, and empathetic
Sharp differentiation between work and private life	=>	Work and private life intermingle
Hierarchy, pyramids	=>	Projects, networks, flatter organizations
"Do as I say"	=>	Leading by example, lives as one teaches

When many associates approach or enjoy the post-conventional range of individual growth, the organization spontaneously extends towards a *visionary* and value-based perspective, with focus on meaning or "why." Here we find an advanced corporate culture where healthy attitudes and sound human values are lively throughout the organization. Each associate's personal development is important—the idea is that if the members are happy and engaged, then the organization will automatically do well. Such organizations emphasize mutual respect and tolerance, nourishing feelings, equality, trust, freedom under responsibility, dynamism, entrepreneurship, independent perspectives, looking for problems (i.e., new business ideas), the prevention of conflicts and failures, and creative conflict resolution. Typically, we find clearly articulated core purpose (mission), core values, and goals. The associates are genuinely concerned with such healthy human values as morals, fairness, beauty, and enhancing the environment. Good luck and fortunate coincidences are common. With humor, it has been said about a value-driven airline that "attitude is more important than altitude."

Value-based organizations are characterized by good communication and open sharing of information throughout the organization. We find a welcoming of honest feedback, win-win interpersonal strategies, and empowered associates who thrive on high performance demands and standards. The high quality products and services tend to be innovative and in the forefront of research and development. We thus find high levels of success along with high levels of satisfaction throughout the company.

Soft versus hard management. Post-conventional organizations tend to employ soft management practice. Several meta-analyses—which bring together research on hundreds of thousands of people—conclude that soft management is much more effective than hard management in terms of productivity and profitability, both on the individual and collective level (Humphrey et al., 2007; Rich et al., 2010). The post-conventional, humanistic perspective of soft management achieves results through consensus-based decisions, widespread focus on delegation and self-management, high member participation and freedom, high trust, extensive training and development at all organizational levels, promotion from within the organization, high job security, supporting associates, high fixed salary, meaningful work, and high-performance work practices.

In contrast, hard management means hard work, many external controls and incentive systems, excessive focus on money, and that the return on investment to the owners is the primary (sometimes even only) objective for doing business, corresponding to conventional organizations.

For individuals it is not possible to live the reality of a level of development above that where they are (Torbert, 1991). Similarly, an organization cannot enact the reality of a higher level of collective consciousness than the one it possesses, i.e., conventional organizations cannot enact the features of post-conventional organizations. Let us draw a parallel to the prefrontal cortex—the CEO of the brain. If the typical organizational member has a conventional development, their "internal CEO" is not able to lead them in a satisfactory way, and they instead need an external CEO to guide them. Thus, a softer, more advanced style of management, based on autonomous members, will only work in an organization where the level of collective consciousness is high enough. The *situational leadership theory* echoes this contingency: The most successful leaders are those that adapt their leadership style to the maturity of the individual or group they are attempting to lead or influence (Hersey and Blanchard, 1969).

CHARACTERISTICS OF POST-CONVENTIONAL ORGANIZATIONS

Different individuals and departments carry out different tasks in an organization. With organizations approaching or at the post-conventional level, individuals and departments increasingly function in *alignment* so that they work more and more for the common good. This alignment reduces reliance on controls and extrinsic motivators, and results in higher collective performance. In the natural sciences, alignment is called *coherence*, which also leads to better performance. For instance, the power of a laser beam arises from the photons or light particles being perfectly coherent. Recall that more coherent brain functioning was seen in high-performing individuals in sports and management compared to average-performing controls.

Visionary companies are to a considerable extent able to satisfy *all* stakeholders: Associates, management, customers, suppliers, and shareholders. They also contribute constructively to society, i.e., exercising sound corporate social responsibility. Such high-performing corporations may even work to support competitors, e.g., Toyota holding seminars for competitors about its pioneering production methods (Taylor, 1997).

When compared to conventional organizations, post-conventional organizations can be summed up by two themes: (1) "putting man before money"—the happiness and well-being of associates are more important than profit, and (2) the ability to be effective, which is to "do less and accomplish more." An example of this higher effectiveness is that the Baldrige Award companies in the USA spend 80–85 percent of their time on non-urgent but important tasks, while organizations performing on a substantially lower level spend much more time on urgent but non-important tasks (Covey, 2009).

Ethics and Performance. Post-conventional collective development has implications for the ethical climate and performance of organizations. Recall that world-class athletes, top-level managers, and professional classical musicians—merely selected based on the level of their performance—exhibited significantly higher moral reasoning than their average-performing controls. This suggests "morality pays" on the individual level. Similarly, organizations based on sound human values and ethics over time tend to outperform organizations where these features are less pronounced, e.g., there is a link between corporate social responsibility and different measures of corporate financial performance (Dam, 2006). The corporation G. C. Rieber in Bergen, Norway, has been successful for over 130 years. Throughout this time its first commercial principle has been "The company shall not do any business that is not assessed as advantageous to both the buyer and the seller." This win-win thinking represents both a moral principle and a business success principle.

Unfortunately, conventional thinking dominates in today's collective consciousness: Health care focuses on treatment, not prevention. Politics is primarily a win-lose game, not win-win. Law and ethical rules emphasize punishing those who are caught, i.e., "who can we blame?" Since unethical behavior is recurring all the time, there is little progress in terms of "what can we learn?"

When conventional thinking dominates, lower-level ethics are common, e.g., cheating, bribing, or misuse of funds. With only 10 percent of the population in the post-conventional range, we can understand why there are few ethical thinkers on Wall Street. Similarly, we can appreciate why Henrik Ibsen—an internationally acclaimed author—in the drama *An Enemy of the People* wrote: "The most dangerous enemy of the truth and freedom amongst us is the compact majority."

How does conventional thinking grip an organization? Brain research shows that due to the powerful influence of peer pressure it is a challenge for an individual to think independently from the surrounding collective mentality (Mauboussin, 2009). When a person tries to think independently from peer pressure, there is an increase in the activity of the fear center of the brain. Thus social pressure can even make a person say something they know to be false. Even those participants in this research who remained independent in their thinking had higher activity in the fear center when questioning the pervasive world-view. This illustrates the power of collective consciousness.

It continues to be a problem that the establishment resists fundamental progress, i.e., Galileo's claim that the sun was at the center of our solar system met with 400 years of opposition. Fortunately, as individual and collective consciousness now rise to a post-conventional reality, it is becoming easier for the individual to think independently, and increasingly acceptable to society that individuals do so.

ORGANIZATIONAL STRUCTURE AND LEVEL OF COLLECTIVE CONSCIOUSNESS

People with higher mind-brain development have attributes like self-esteem, humbleness, lovingness, and objectivity. Since they are intrinsically motivated, external rank is not important. Instead equality and focus on what needs to be done will dominate.

For many years, there has been a trend in the West to encourage post-conventional properties such as equality, self-management, self-organization, and flatter organizations in order to improve performance. Such initiatives will in particular be an advantage in the modern high-competency knowledge organizations, where it is impossible for the formal leader to master all the different specialized areas. Instead, the leadership role often rotates between the associates depending on who has most knowledge in the area considered at any time. Some organizations are even working to do away with leaders and job titles in the traditional sense, such as the Las Vegas–based company Zappos with 1500 associates and over 24 million customers. Here is a description of the type of equality and distributed leadership that we expect to find in post-conventional organizations (Sjøvold and Hovden, cited by Evensen, 2009a):

> *The dynamics of creative groups are characterized by equal contributions by the members, and that they have equal status and power of influence in relation to both the group and decisions. In fact, we saw that strong leadership whereby someone "takes charge" hampered creativity. In mature groups, the roles are not static and fixed, but fluid and adaptive. In this way, such groups are better able to meet the challenges they face. In such well-performing groups the members' roles change based on what the group at any time needs.*

Even in post-conventional organizations there may be factors limiting extensive self-management. First, some people seem to have a natural inclination to serve and to be directed. Second, when a group requires extensive coordination, such as when performing tasks that call for interdependence among the group members, hierarchy wins out (Galinsky et al., 2012). Third, the extent of hierarchy may at least in part be culturally dependent. While flatter organizational structures are an advantage in many Western countries, a hierarchy could give best performance in certain Eastern countries like China (Yang, 2012). We summarize the question of flat or hierarchical organizations:

1. High mind-brain development in all associates is more important than the organizational design.
2. With higher levels of collective consciousness the range of organizational structures will increase, just like individuals through development increasingly become more their unique selves—and thus distinct from anybody else.
3. With higher collective mind-brain development, the most optimal organizational structure will naturally unfold depending on such factors as the tendencies and likes and dislikes of the people involved, the type and size of business, the nature of the task, and the national cultures that are involved. Thus various degrees of flatness or hierarchy can be expected within the general trend towards more self-management suggested by the four levels of organizational development that we have outlined.

Illustrations of Post-conventional Organizations

What would organizations look like that are approaching or have reached post-conventional levels of collective consciousness? Such organizations might have attributes like extensive self-management, purpose beyond profits, long-term perspective, and lively healthy values. They are typically featured on "best places to work" lists. To illustrate the theory, we first consider a selection of large, visionary corporations that have been in operation for on average over 110 years, thus backing that post-conventional attributes support long-term success. Then, we explore three young, high-performing organizations that display several post-conventional attributes: The Norwegian national women's handball team; the Sky Factory, Iowa; and Nordic Naturals, California.

A. EIGHTEEN VISIONARY COMPANIES

Instead of being interested in what is new, we ought to be interested in what is true.

— Pfeffer's Law (Pfeffer and Sutton, 2006, p. 29)

The book *Built to Last* considers 18 visionary or value-based companies such as Minnesota Mining and Manufacturing (3M), IBM, Johnson & Johnson, Procter & Gamble, General Electric, Walt Disney, and Ford (Collins and Porras, 2002). These visionary companies were selected based on a survey of 1,000 CEOs who ranked companies using the following criteria: (1) a premier institution in its industry, (2) widely admired by knowledgeable businesspeople, (3) had made an indelible imprint on the world, (4) had multiple generations of CEOs, (5) had multiple product/service life cycles, and (6) was founded before 1950.

The visionary companies were compared to 18 similar but less visionary companies. The performance of both groups of companies was assessed using the growth in share value. During 64 years, from 1926 to 1990, the share value of the visionary companies increased by almost 8 times that of the control companies, and by 16 times the USA stock market index.

There appears to be several post-conventional human values or principles lively in most of the high-performing companies, such as (1) clock building, not time telling: Have focus on the long-term building of the organization, not on the leader or any one product; (2) more than profits: Sound human values are primary; (3) preserve the core and stimulate progress: Perhaps the most important principle; (4) home-grown management: Promote from within; and (5) aligning the associates with the company's vision: Goal, core purpose, and core values.

As noted, any organizational culture has a tendency not to change, despite associates' coming and going. This coexistence of change and non-change is similar to a river that remains the same even though the water molecules come and go. Poorly performing businesses may be forced out of business at an early stage. In contrast, due to the high performance of visionary companies, they tend to last long. A long life span is therefore an indication of an advanced organizational culture. The concept of collective consciousness sheds light on several of the advanced features found in visionary companies:

- Emphasis on building the organization: Create a high-level collective consciousness, the prime mover of an organization.

- Focus on the whole organization, not on the leader: The leader is a reflection of collective consciousness.

- Promote from within: Once a high level of collective consciousness has been established, it is vital to maintain it.

- Good enough never is: No matter how far the visionary companies are ahead of their competitors, they never give up the quest for continuous improvement, indicating that growth-orientation and intrinsic motivation are lively.

Recall that luck often is a contributor to individual success. On the organizational level, strategy routinely explains less than one-half of the performance variance across firms (Morgan and Rego, 2009); the rest may involve luck. There are many examples of how visionary companies virtually stumbled across new business opportunities. For example, one associate of 3M was singing in a choir and used small pieces of paper to mark the chosen songs in her songbook. However, the paper pieces had a tendency to fall out. One day she ran into a colleague who had invented glue that did not dry. The result was *Post-it* notes, a world success.

What has happened to the 18 visionary companies since the study was completed in 1994? On a 2012 list of the greenest companies in the USA, two of the visionary corporations—IBM and HP—were ranked first and second, and 10 of them were amongst the top 50 (Newsweek, 2012). Almost half of these companies (including IBM, General Electric, Sony, and Ford) were ranked amongst the 50 most innovative companies globally in 2010 (Bloomberg.com, 2011).

And what about financial performance? Despite individual ups and downs, the visionary companies as a whole continued to perform on a high level from 1994 to 2004 (Reingold and Underwood, 2004). From August 1994 to August 2004 their average stock value increased by 206 percent, compared to 132 percent for the USA Standard & Poor stock index. For the nine comparison companies that still were on the stock exchange in 2004, the average share value increased by only 32 percent in this period. The remaining nine comparison companies had either been sold or gone bankrupt.

The older an organization is, the more likely it is that its level of collective consciousness will change towards (equilibrium with) that of its surrounding society. Since the visionary companies already on average are more than 110 years old, it is possible that sooner or later some of these organizations will shift towards an average level of performance in their societies.

B. NORWEGIAN NATIONAL WOMEN'S HANDBALL TEAM

The Norwegian national women's handball team is the first example of a small, relatively young organization with many post-conventional features. During the period 1994–2009, when the team was led by the female coach Marit Breivik, it won a total of six gold medals: One Olympic championship, one world championship, and four European championships. In addition, the team secured five silver and two bronze medals in these championships—altogether 13 medals in 15 years (Hole, 2009). This is the most successful performance period of any Norwegian national team, whether men or women. As could be expected, the high performance level *has* persisted after Marit resigned as the coach.

In line with other organizations having post-conventional features, Marit worked towards the players taking a high degree of responsibility—she wanted "involved players." Without hesitation, she says that the most important thing she did as a coach was to "contribute to giving the players insight into themselves" (Myklemyr, 2008). Over the years, Marit increasingly realized that the players must assume responsibility for the team—as a collective undertaking. Teamwork was often used during training, and the players had a lot of freedom to develop the play. For example, one group determined how the defensive play was to be organized while another group considered what was important to have in mind during attacks. She continues, "Often it is what goes on inside the heads of the players which makes the difference between victory and loss" (Myklemyr, 2001).

Marit was present and involved in all group work, because "in some situations they need my acceptance and support." She continues: "As coach you are not present in the duels on the court. The players must have confidence in their own skills. My job is to raise their level of feeling secure." Accordingly, in line with the visionary organizations described above, she is not promoting herself, but the team—"clock building, not time telling."

Other values lively in the team were focus on excellence and the positive. When a new player entered the team, she was asked to make a list of her strengths. There was only this one list; the new player was not asked to list her weaknesses. Excellence in a task means that the underlying brain circuits are functioning well. By repeating the successful action, these circuits are further reinforced, leading to self-confidence and a positive experience. The alternative of focusing on weaknesses reinforces brain circuits which are working in an unsatisfactory way. Marit Breivik explains this strength-based management:

> *We chose to put more emphasis on what each player was good at. We were very concrete and wanted in this way to improve the players' self-insight. Before one can make demands, one has to build up the self-confidence of each player.*

Marit selected strong and different personalities for her team, and she wanted to show that it was acceptable to be different. She is convinced that each player can have her own personal style without being in conflict with the team, i.e., that "unity in diversity" is an optimal scenario. She was concerned with developing her players. It is important for each player to survey herself in order to know herself better. During important matches Marit placed the best players amongst the spectators, this was to stimulate more players to rise to the occasion. She reasoned that if she had only used the best players, the team would have become very vulnerable. This reflects long-term, holistic, and proactive thinking. Marit Breivik also says to succeed the players must function as "whole human beings," i.e., there must be harmony between the sport, education, hobbies, and family, a further sign of a more comprehensive strategy. She notes, "If you look at the wholeness you in addition get unlimited potential for development."

The Norwegian weekly management newspaper *Ukeavisen Ledelse* honored Marit Breivik by giving her the Good Leadership Award for 2007. When accepting this award, she summed up her leadership philosophy in the following way:

> *Leadership is not about having as many people under you as possible or as much money as possible to look after. Leadership is about getting the best out of your associates, about loyalty, wisdom, and boldness. Leadership is about being devoted to a mission and being fond of those people you are collaborating with.*

In conclusion, during Marit's coaching period of the Norwegian national women's handball team there were several collective attributes reflecting a post-conventional organization, such as

- Inclusive leadership style.
- Players responsible for their own development.

- Participative decision-making.

C. THE SKY FACTORY, FAIRFIELD, IOWA, USA

"The purpose of our business is to enrich and sustain life."

In 2002, at the age of 60, Bill Witherspoon founded the Sky Factory. The business idea is to incorporate illusions of nature in enclosed interiors—areas in a building that are far removed from external walls—which lack the restorative qualities of views of nature. Healthcare facilities represent the largest market. Open sky compositions and real-time digital cinema audio-visual content are incorporated into a skylight framework to create illusory skies or virtual windows to display panoramic views. The benefits of these installations in reducing stress and anxiety is well supported by empirical research.

However, Bill's deeper motivation was to design a "beautiful corporation." Previously, he had been the entrepreneur of several companies. Yet he did not feel he had created a successful organizational or management structure, much less a company culture that properly supported all the parties of a successful business—customers, employees, investors, and founders. To realize this desire he turned the Sky Factory into a creative experiment.

According to Bill, culture is to the corporation what DNA is to the life of living organisms—the internal blueprint that guides healthy functioning. Therefore, he built the Sky Factory around five cultural principles, which gave rise to its organizational blueprint or corporate "DNA":

1. *Transparency.* All information throughout the company is open and displayed to all staff with the exception of individual HR matters and individual compensation. Weekly all-company meetings include review of current company financials and performance metrics, as well as discussion of all significant short- and long-term business issues and decisions.

2. *Flat management.* Sky Factory does not have a hierarchical system of management—no managers or supervisors apart from a president and a CEO. It is a "horizontal" organization of self-motivated, networking individuals who participate in multiple job-teams. Each person takes periodic responsibility as the "facilitator" for one or more functional groups. Because all information is uniformly distributed, power is also located everywhere—rather

than being concentrated in the hands of a few. Individuals rotating through different jobs and teams, as well as transparency, support this goal. The flat management is described by Aaron Birlson, staff since 2004:

> *Nobody and everybody is my boss. You don't report to anybody, but you report to everybody. ... I was glad to leave the 'us versus them' mentality behind when I came to the Sky Factory.*

3. *Consensus.* All business decisions are made by consensus—either within small teams or by the entire company. Transparency and alertness to the full range of the company's goals and business activities, combined with flat management, ensure that gaining consensus is highly efficient. Consensus ensures that all decisions reflect the group's collective intelligence and results in maximum buy-in and engagement. In the interest of dynamic forward movement, the president and CEO can, if needed, break standstills or bottlenecks should they occur.

4. *Service.* Bill notes that service is the foundation that underlies the relationship of all Sky Factory members with each other and with customers, the corporation, and the community. In one way or another, everyone takes care of each other. This kind of service is contractual. However, it has become increasingly common that many find themselves engaging in service spontaneously—without consideration of return. This type of "selfless" service transforms the workplace towards an ideal environment.

5. *Performance.* Individual, team, and corporate performance (aesthetic, quality, ethical, and financial) are the criteria used for evaluation. Everyone at Sky Factory asks one question: Since this is my company, how should I perform?

Individual compensation (i.e., salary, profit sharing, and company ownership) is performance-based. The salary range is only 2.8 to 1. Profit sharing, calculated as 50 percent of net profit, accounts for at least one third of total compensation and is distributed monthly. All full-time staff participate in a performance-based ownership plan designed to redistribute the company ownership to a 40 percent employee, 30 percent investor, and 30 percent founder split.

In the flat organization, it is essential to employ only people that *fit* into the organization culture. In the beginning, only conventional means of selection were used. This resulted in an annual turnover of around 33 percent. Consequently, the hiring procedure was revised. Now, the hiring process includes 18 interviews done by associates from throughout the company. Each interview relies on two elements: Intuition and analysis. Intuition assesses how the individual fits with the culture. Analysis assesses whether they have suitable skills and personality traits. This hiring protocol has resulted in a 3 percent turnover in recent years.

There are many post-conventional organizational features in the Sky Factory culture:

1. Equality, win-win assumptions, mutual support, consensus, transparency, free flow of information, and job rotation.

2. Flat management and network: Self-management, self-motivated employees, and high engagement.

3. Effective members throughout, shared vision, few and simple rules, coexistence of freedom and ethical behavior.

The Sky Factory has enjoyed substantial growth every year—as illustrated by the growth in revenue shown in Table 5.2—and had 40 employees as of August 2013. Bill hopes his company will be a model for future organizations. He believes the twenty-first century will bring increasing demand for corporate cultures that support and bring out the best in everybody.

Table 5.2 Growth in Revenue for the Sky Factory

From One Year to the Next	Growth in Revenue (Percentage)
2006–2007	13.7
2007–2008	21.5
2008–2009	5.2
2009–2010	4.0
2010–2011	25.4
2011–2012	11.9
2012–2013	1.3

D. NORDIC NATURALS, WATSONVILLE, CALIFORNIA, USA

> *Sustainable development is development that meets the needs of the present without compromising the ability of future generations to meet their own needs.*
>
> — Brundtland Commission of the United Nations (March 20, 1987)

Joar Opheim comes from Bodø, a small town in northern Norway, where fish and fish oil are part of daily life. Joar completed his MBA in the USA and then worked for several years in Silicon Valley. During this time, he was unable to find the high-quality fish oil he relied on to manage his old gymnastic injuries, and he had to bring bottles back from Norway—filling his suitcase during every return trip. To meet this need, Joar started his own omega-3 company, Nordic Naturals, in 1995 in a 150 sq. ft. bedroom in California. The goal was "to eliminate the omega-3 deficiency around the world, while applying the highest level of ethical business principles and environmentalism in the process."

Today, the company is a leading global manufacturer of omega-3 products, with 51 percent of the market in the USA. Its headquarters are an 85,000 sq. ft. LEED Gold certified building in Watsonville, and the company has approximately 300 associates in the USA and 30 in Norway. During all of Nordic Naturals' 18 years of operation, the annual growth in revenues has been between 10 and 100 percent.

Nordic Naturals and its products have received over 30 awards for taste and product excellence. For example, in 2010, *Vitamin Retailer Magazine* named the company Manufacturer of the Year, recognizing its excellence in five key areas:

1. Quality.
2. Leadership in science.
3. Leadership in innovation.
4. Respect for the environment.
5. Dedication to retailers and the natural products industry.

Sound human values have been at the core of Nordic Naturals right from the start. These values exemplify features of a post-conventional organization, such as leading by example, high integrity, growth-orientation, and high trust. The work environment is informal with a sense of equality. This culture supports open channels of communication in which employees can work efficiently with others and feel free to bring new ideas to the table in an effort to remain innovative and competitive.

There is little direct oversight within departments, as employees are given the responsibility to understand their roles within the larger context of the company and to manage their share of work. Quarterly reviews delivered by the CEO include information on company progress, placement in the market, sales, product innovation, and company vision. This free exchange of information builds morale at Nordic Naturals by giving direct feedback to employees in the context of the success and challenges faced by the company. Most importantly, employees' work is validated by profit sharing tied to quarterly sales and divided equally amongst *all* associates. This reinforces the understanding that company success is the product of shared responsibility and collective efforts across departments, with the overarching aim of producing exceptional products and excellent customer service.

Stage 4. Consciousness-based: Higher States of Collective Consciousness

By higher states of collective consciousness we mean a level of collective growth beyond post-conventional. In these most advanced organizations and societies, what matters most is the development of individual and collective consciousness. Such collective realities arise when a sufficient proportion of the members are enjoying higher states of (individual) consciousness.

Regular contact with Transcendental Consciousness by a sufficient number of associates is predicted to enliven the experience of "wholeness" throughout the organization. This mature growth will be reflected in higher-order attributes that provide the foundation for lasting collective peak performance. Examples of such advanced attributes are (1) complete integration of all the different components and activities of the organization—wholeness on the move, (2) behavior in accordance with natural law, including the law of least action—do least and accomplish most, and (3) organization-wide excellence. Table 5.3 contrasts post-conventional organizations with those in higher states of collective consciousness.

Table 5.3 Contrasting Post-conventional Organizations with Organizations in Higher States of Collective Consciousness

Post-conventional Organizations	Organizations in Higher States of Collective Consciousness
Self-actualization and frequent peak experiences the norm for the associates	Higher consciousness the norm for the associates
Do less and accomplish more	Do least and accomplish most
Considerable happiness amongst associates	Associates enjoying stable bliss
Value-based performance	Natural law–based performance
Effective organizations	World-class organizations
Alignment through shared goals, core values, and core purpose	Alignment with holistic intelligence of nature
Engages human intelligence—lower self	Engages the managing intelligence of nature—higher Self
Empowerment	Management by automation
Self-sufficiency	Sense of invincibility
Sound ethics, internalizing what is right and wrong	Compassion for all life
Win-win interpersonal strategies	All good for everyone—no good for no one
Impulse to act: Unfulfilled desires triggered by current events	Fulfillment: Action satisfies the need of the time, i.e., timely action
Temporary peak performance	Lasting peak performance
World-class performance in narrow domains	Generalized world-class performance in a wide range of activities
Peak performance for relatively simple tasks	Peak performance for both simple and complex tasks
Consciousness mainly aware of objects	Consciousness aware of both itself and objects
Activity causes wear and tear on body and mind	Activity in accordance with the law of least action
Actualizes individual potential	Actualizes nature's potential

Because peak experiences are spontaneous and not systematically available, there are still very few people in the world enjoying stabilized higher consciousness. This shortage on the individual level explains why even glimpses of higher states of collective consciousness—what we may call a collective peak experience—are rare today. At the beginning of this chapter, we cited a collective peak experience enjoyed by the eminent basketball player Bill Russell and the Boston Celtics. Below, we cite further such shared experiences from sports and music together with a study that found interpersonal brain integration in musicians playing together.

A. COLLECTIVE PEAK EXPERIENCE IN A SPORTS TEAM

Susann Goksør Bjerkrheim—who played for the Norwegian women's handball team under Marit Breivik's leadership—describes a typical collective peak experience. This kind of experience she enjoyed many times when playing for a junior team, a senior team, and the national team:

> *Sometimes, all the way from the warm-up the communication with the other team members is good, and you know in advance that today you are going to succeed in an unbelievable way. On such days, there is a shared, positive mood in the team. It is abstract and gives energy. I feel the response from others. Everybody is fully present in the situation. There is a mass suggestive effect where we all melt into a greater fellowship. I get chills down my spine. I feel world-class when this community mood is there—a strong togetherness or coherence. During such exhilarated times, when things fall into place … the action of each player is extremely well coordinated with those of all the other players. There is rhythm and harmony in the team. We read each other correctly, things float, and there is a high spirit and energy. Everybody contributes her energy into the team. Definitely extreme energy is created.*
>
> *It is difficult to recreate this mood—either it is there or it is not there. We know a lot about the characteristics of this shared mood: Deep eye contact, extreme presence. We try to recreate, but it may not come. This shared mood must come from within each player. It has to be genuine. It comes by itself—accidentally. Absolutely it is a collective high—much stronger than an individual high. Everybody has to be fully present. If one player is not fully there, this may disturb … it is also expanded to include the spectators. Yes, there is a tense energy. The mood characterizes the whole sports hall. It is intense; some people have to leave. There is a kick.*

Notice in this quotation that all the particulars of the competition are experienced in high detail. Yet the boundaries between the individual players are secondary; even the individual sense of self is secondary. What is primary is the flow of each player in an orchestrated *whole*. The team moves like one person.

Susann's experience contains several other qualities described in this book as belonging to excellent performance, including qualities echoing the three components of the Brain Integration Scale:

- *Coherence.* " … communication with the other team members is good. … [W]e all melt into a greater fellowship. … I feel world-class when this community mood is there—a strong togetherness or coherence. … [T]he action of each player is extremely well coordinated with those of all the other players. … There is rhythm and harmony in the team."

- *Alertness.* "Everybody is fully present in the situation. … [E]xtreme presence. … Absolutely it is a collective high."

- *Economy of action.* "During such exhilarated times, when things fall into place. … We read each other correctly, things float … "

- *Happiness.* "On such days there is a shared, positive mood in the team. … I get chills down my spine. … During such exhilarated times."

- *Whole is more than collection of parts.* "Absolutely it is a collective high—much stronger than an individual high. … If one player is not fully there, this may disturb."

- *Vitality.* "Definitely extreme energy is created. … On such days, there is a shared, positive mood in the team. It is abstract and gives energy. … Yes, there is a tense energy."

- *Sense of invincibility.* " … you know in advance that today you are going to succeed in an unbelievable way."

- *Consciousness as a field.* "The mood characterizes the whole sports hall."

B. COLLECTIVE PEAK EXPERIENCE IN AN ORCHESTRA

> *Sometimes during a performance [in an orchestra] … you can feel that everybody is focused; it becomes easy, as if all of us suddenly became one body where all the parts are working perfectly together, everybody breathes together, everything becomes one big energy, and everything feels crystal clear, like the brains/souls of everybody melt together and want the same. It doesn't matter if you play the oboe or triangle, or conduct. … I feel a direct mental connection with both any co-musicians and members of the audience. A very real contact. However, I'm thinking*

> *very little about the others in the room. (Thoughts that otherwise can be present: "Do they like what I'm doing?" and performance-anxiety, etc. are totally gone.) The only thing that is important is the music. Who is there, and what they are, think of me—everything like that disappears. I only feel their and my own mental presence.*
>
> — Anna Skogman, professional violin player, The Norwegian Opera

Notice in this quotation the statement "as if all of us suddenly became one body where all the parts are working perfectly together ... brains/souls of everybody melt together and want the same." Again, the distinction between individual players and musical sections is in the background. What is most alive is the "direct mental connection with both any co-musicians and members of the audience." Thus, the *wholeness* of the performance is what is most salient, and it integrates all the parts into the music: "The only thing that is important is the music."

C. INTERPERSONAL BRAIN INTEGRATION IN MUSICIANS

We have seen that individual brain integration is fundamental to individual peak experiences and high performance. Similarly, scientists at the Max Planck Institute in Germany have found interpersonal brain integration amongst musicians playing together (Lindenberger et al., 2009). The study considered eight groups of two guitarists playing a short jazz-fusion melody together up to 60 times. It was found that the players' brains became synchronized in the same fashion as their instruments. The similarities among the brain wave phases—both within and between the brains of the musicians—increased significantly both during a metronome beat in preparation for playing and when the musicians actually played together. The brains' frontal and central regions showed the strongest synchronization patterns, but the back regions also showed relatively high synchronization in at least half of the pairs of musicians.

Summarizing this Chapter

This chapter has examined the fourth dimension of the Unified Theory of Performance—the influence on individual performance of the stage of development of the different units of collective consciousness in which the performer operates. We presented several novel ideas. First, the real mover of an organization or a society is the underlying stage of collective consciousness, which is formed by the stage of mind-brain development of all members. We described a model of development of collective consciousness, and four stages were discussed in detail: Conventional (lower and upper), post-conventional, and higher states of collective consciousness. Several examples of high-performing, post-conventional organizations were presented.

Second, we argued that the leader is a reflection of the level of collective consciousness. This principle means that the leader cannot achieve more than the followers deserve. Third, we noted that any organization can reach excellence through a collective peak experience, a wholeness that seems to be much stronger and more life-supportive than an individual peak experience. Since higher individual consciousness is still rare, we could only present a few collective peak experiences. Having discussed the four dimensions of performance in the previous four chapters, we will bring them together in the next chapter in the Unified Theory of Performance.

Chapter 6

The Performeasure® Assessment—Revealing the Secret of World-class Performance

A theory is the more impressive the greater is the simplicity of its premises, the more different are the kinds of things it relates, and the more extended the range of its applicability.

— Albert Einstein

In India, there is a story of an elephant that once came to a village during a very dark night. Some people touched the side of the elephant and said it was a wall; some gripped a leg and said it was a tree trunk; and some touched the ear, concluding that it was a leaf. Everybody was right, only the big picture was missing! This story is analogous to current recommendations to improve performance: Some schools emphasize physical training, others extensive practice, mental training, more education, or copying those who have been successful. However, the different schools usually do not consider each other's recommendations. This chapter outlines a comprehensive model of performance that unifies the different approaches by including the common, underlying, and essential factor of mind-brain development.

Unified Theory of Performance

The previous four chapters considered separately the four dimensions of high performance—integrated brain functioning, higher psychological development, higher consciousness, and higher levels of collective consciousness, as shown in Figure 6.1. The present chapter integrates these four dimensions into the Unified Theory of Performance, which states that higher mind-brain development provides the basis of higher performance in any profession or field of activity.

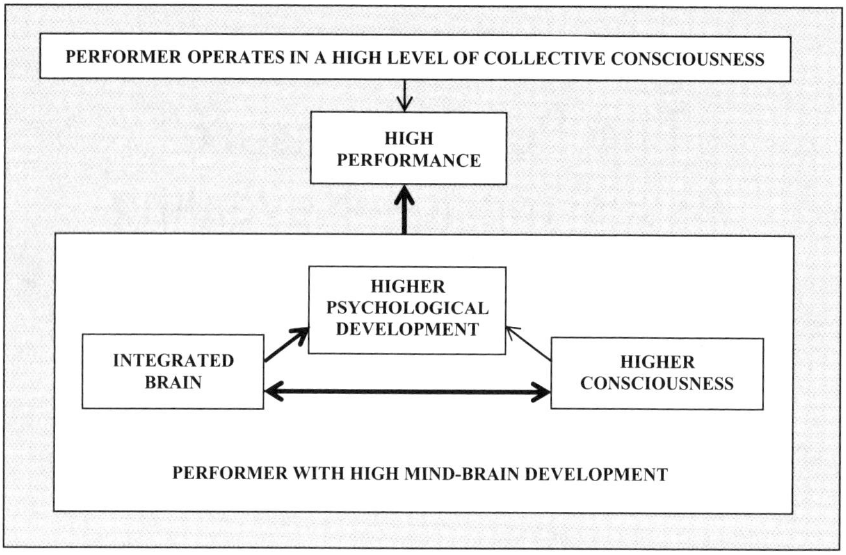

Figure 6.1 Unified Theory of Performance and High Performance

The Unified Theory of Performance predicts that highly successful people should have higher levels of mind-brain development than average-performing individuals. Higher levels of mind-brain development would allow high performers to see a creative solution to difficult problems in society; to see the opportunity to gain a competitive advantage in any sport; and to enrich and master any vocation. Our four studies presented earlier support this prediction. The following equation captures this theory:

$$\text{Individual performance} \approx f(\text{brain integration, psychological development, higher consciousness, level of collective consciousness}) \quad (6.1)$$

The first three factors refer to individual development, while the level of collective consciousness includes the influence of family, friends, team(s), organization(s), city, nation, and world. The individual level of mind-brain development is a larger predictor of individual performance than the level of collective consciousness—even within challenging socioeconomic environments, world-class performers do emerge.

INDIVIDUAL MIND-BRAIN SYNERGY

The four dimensions of the Unified Theory of Performance work *synergistically* to determine the quality of performance, as shown in Figure 6.1. Brain development is the core of the theory. For the individual, higher brain integration strongly supports higher psychological development and more frequent glimpses of higher consciousness, as shown by the thick arrows. Higher consciousness in turn reinforces different sets of favorable brain circuits and positively influences higher psychological development. However, we do not think that higher psychological development in a significant way directly feeds back into brain integration and higher consciousness. This synergistic activity of mind and brain is seen by the correlation between different measures of psychophysiology reported in our studies of peak performers:

- *Athletes*: We found positive correlations between the Brain Integration Scale scores and moral reasoning. In addition, ego or self-development correlated with two variables on the Survey of Peak Experiences: Question 1 (Transcendental experiences during eyes closed relaxation) and Question 2 (Transcendental experiences during waking activity).

- *Managers*: There were positive correlations between scores on the Brain Integration Scale, luck, and moral reasoning.

- *Musicians*: Scores on the Brain Integration Scale positively correlated with frequency of peak experiences during waking activity and moral reasoning. In addition, faster resolution of response conflict on the Stroop test correlated with higher scores on moral reasoning.

Other studies have also found a correlation between the three individual performance dimensions. Teenagers having above-average IQs have higher levels of neural connections in the frontal brain areas (Petsche, 1996), and higher brain wave coherence is associated with higher creativity (Benedek et al., 2011). In musicians and visual artists reporting peak moments, the range of such experiences triggered for the individual was significantly correlated with self-actualization, but there was no correlation with respondents' age, sex, education, and visual art or music ability (Panzarella, 1980). Maslow found that the closer a person came to self-actualization, the more peak experiences he or she reported. As shown in research on 21 successful product-development engineers at Volvo in Sweden, higher flexibility and originality in verbal and figural creativity tests were positively correlated with higher levels of brain integration, faster brain processing, faster speed of decision-making, and a sense of being in control of one's situation (Travis and Lagrosen, 2014).

UNITS OF COLLECTIVE CONSCIOUSNESS IMPACT INDIVIDUAL PERFORMANCE

The level of development of different units of collective consciousness that we are embedded in also influences our performance. This applies in particular to the family we are born into and the one we establish ourselves as an adult. A family can, for example, buffer the effects of stress on the individual, e.g., a loving mother can buffer effects of early childhood trauma that would normally handicap a person's thinking and feeling (Luby et al., 2012). People we associate with—such as friends, teams, and organizations—have a lesser but nevertheless significant influence on our performance. The largest units of collective consciousness—city, nation, and world—have the least influence on our well-being and behavior.

The collective dimension in Equation 6.1 may explain why home wins are more common than away wins in sports. For example, in soccer the many supporters for the home team give a much stronger, positive collective influence on their team's performance than the fewer supporters for the visiting team. During the 2012–2013 Premier League in soccer in England, 15 of the 20 teams had better records at home than away. The corresponding scenario in Spain was 17 out of 20 teams (Atkins, 2013).

The social context may also explain why peak experiences and the resulting extraordinary performances often take place when there is a substantial supportive audience, e.g., during major sports championships, musicians performing for a large audience, or managers giving presentations to a large group of people.

Several studies have documented the organizational and societal benefits resulting from relatively few of the members practicing meditation (see Chapter 7). This adds further support to the theory that there is a link between individual development and behavior and the level of collective consciousness within which individuals operate.

Higher Individual Mind-brain Development and Excellence

Let us elaborate on the influence your level of mind-brain development has on your level of performance. Mind-brain development supports greater breadth and depth of awareness. You are diving deeper within to be more successful on the outside. As the screen of awareness becomes more lively and comprehensive, you are able to see more opportunities in your life. In addition, you are able to place individual experiences into a larger picture, and are less caught up in the ups and downs of day-to-day events. The context of experiences has changed!

Higher growth facilitates win-win solutions and co-evolution; such individuals will focus on the needs of others, for in supporting others, they support themselves. Furthermore, highly developed individuals are intrinsically and not extrinsically motivated. As a result, they will tend to not be concerned with whether they are well-known in society. There are many examples of highly accomplished leaders who remained anonymous because their focus was on building their organization and not on promoting themselves (Collins and Porras, 2002). Some highly developed people will want to choose a profession or activity where they are less exposed to attention from society, e.g., homemaking, servant, and informal leader. The essential thing is that attaining higher consciousness will naturally result in higher self-referral happiness—the most important aspect of life.

Mind-brain development underlies all skills and so is the common key to develop excellence in all domains of life. Thus, while practice may allow you to develop specific skills, transforming mind and brain allows you to become great. So to be successful you need to focus on both inner growth and outer activities. If you want to be a great piano player, you still need to practice the piano. However, with greater mind-brain development, you will find you progress more quickly, and the people around you will enjoy the music more.

We maintain that the capacity of people to achieve superlative performance for themselves, and for those they influence, spontaneously and progressively unfolds with human development. This means that mind-brain-development is *the* single factor that unfolds a large spectrum of human attributes that are essential for higher levels of knowledge and skills and for the resultant actualizing of performance. Thus, to accomplish most, to function at optimal levels and meet complex demands, a person must develop this most fundamental level to the highest degree possible.

Predicting Level of Performance

Psychological tests are increasingly in use to create more objectivity in the employment process (Caruth et al., 2009). Three out of four major companies in Norway use psychological testing when engaging a new associate (Skorstad, 2008). However, to get a more reliable assessment of an individual's potential for performance, one could measure more than one performance dimension and include an objective (physiological) measure. In the following, we will first consider how well commonly used intelligence tests predict the performance level, and then move on to our expanded mind-brain assessment.

INTELLIGENCE AND PERFORMANCE

A high IQ is a common feature of persons with extraordinary success, such as Albert Einstein. The higher the IQ is, the better the education, the higher the income, the greater the success, and the longer the life. But, and there is a big but, this applies only up to a certain level. Above 120, the relationship between IQ and success ceases. The psychologist Liam Hudson (Henmo, 2009) concludes that an experienced researcher with an IQ of 130 has the same probability of winning the Nobel Prize as one with 180. To improve the validity of intelligence in predicting level of performance, we therefore need a broader, more practical measure than IQ.

The British psychologist Charles Spearman's (1863–1945) most notable contribution to intelligence testing is the idea that all aspects of intelligence, to a certain extent, are correlated with each other. In particular, Spearman believed that intelligence tests only measures two factors: (1) a general intelligence factor common to all tests, called *g-factor*, and (2) a specific factor that is distinctive in each test (Smith and Smith, 2005). General intelligence is a broad term reflected in the ability to reason, plan, solve problems, think abstractly, understand complex ideas, learn quickly, and make use of experience (Gottfredson, 1997). The existence of one general factor receives support from brain research indicating that the same part of the brain—the prefrontal cortex—is active when a wide range of problems is being solved.

Researchers at the University of Iowa, University of Michigan, and University of Manchester carried out two meta-analyses of millions of adults in thousands of studies spanning up to 90 years of research to explore which human attributes contribute to improved performance (Schmidt and Hunter, 1998; Robertson and Smith, 2001). They summarized the predictive validity for both "overall job performance" and "progress during training" of general intelligence, integrity, and certain other measures, such as on-the-job tests. Their conclusion was that tests involving general intelligence plus integrity offer the best prediction of overall job performance, explaining as much as 42 percent.

Self-control or self-regulation may be a more accurate predictor of performance than intelligence (Baumeister and Tierney, 2011). Increasing levels of self-control result with the shift of reality from object-referral to self-referral that comes with higher psychological development and even more so with higher consciousness. Thus, the research on general intelligence, integrity, and self-control provides support to the more comprehensive Unified Theory of Performance.

Psychological testing methods are usually self-report and so may be biased by knowledge of how the test works. Inclusion of the Brain Integration Scale, an *objective* measure, in the test battery should increase the validity of the selection process. We combined three measures—brain integration, psychological development, and frequency of peak experiences—into a single composite factor called the *Performeasure* assessment.

THE PERFORMEASURE ASSESSMENT

The Performeasure assessment is hypothesized to differentiate top performers from average performers in the same profession, and could also be useful to characterize the nature of different professions. We calculated this measure from the data from our studies of athletes, managers, and musicians:

$$\text{Performeasure assessment} = \text{Brain Integration Scale} + \text{moral reasoning} + \text{Survey of Peak Experiences} + 3 \quad (6.2)$$

We added the factor of 3 to ensure that the Performeasure scores always are above zero. Figure 6.2 presents the score for the three groups. Notice that this measure is significantly higher for the peak performers (darker columns) than for the controls (lighter columns) for all three groups. Also notice that the musicians, as a whole, scored higher than the managers, who were higher than the athletes.

The Performeasure assessment is a single number to help guide selection of candidates for a job or promotion; to assess the impact of education, training, rehabilitation, and health programs; or simply to provide self-insight. Being a composite index, this assessment may be robust against randomly higher or lower values in one of the measures in the assessment. For instance, in the athlete study there were no group differences in frequency of peak experiences, and in the musician study there were no group differences in brain integration. However, when combined in the Performeasure assessment, there were significant differences in all three studies. Thus, this composite index seems to more reliably detect group differences than the individual measures do.

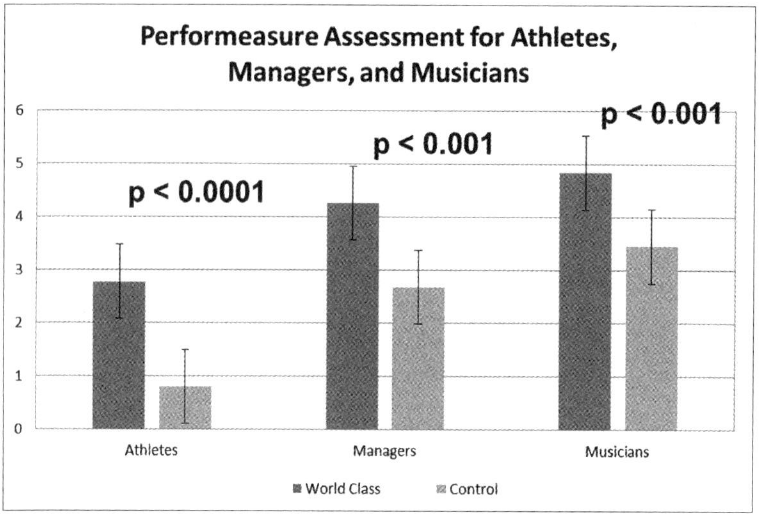

Figure 6.2 The Performeasure Assessment for Athletes, Managers, and Musicians

As seen, general intelligence and integrity have been found to be the best *psychological* predictors of level of performance. Our broader concept of mind-brain development also includes psychological growth, e.g., Gibbs' measure of moral development, which is related to integrity. In additio^{n}, mind-brain development includes levels of brain functioning, which would underlie more effective cognitive and emotional functioning. Future research could compare Performeasure scores to intelligence measures and other tests to determine evidence of validity for this new measure.

Summarizing, the Performeasure assessment appears to satisfy three criteria that are necessary for a general test to predict performance in any vocation or activity: (1) it reflects level of performance in a wide range of activities, (2) it can be reliably measured, and (3) it is robust.

Alternative Factors that May Explain Performance Level

What other factors besides high mind-brain development could explain excellence? We will consider age, education, practice and work experience, incentive programs, and talent and other inborn factors.

1. AGE

The meta-analyses cited above reported that age in *adults* does not correlate with work performance. On average, a 25-year-old and a 55-year-old perform at the same level. Of course, this does not apply to competitive sports, where there is a decline in physical stamina after a certain age. The world-class performers and their controls in each of our three studies were all matched for age, yet the peak performers were more successful. This also removes the effect of age on the level of performance.

The Unified Theory of Performance can explain this stagnation in performance once one reaches adulthood. Based on natural maturation, the mind and brain develop during childhood and youth, resulting in a continuous improvement of performance. However, since individual mind-brain development normally levels off in early adulthood (see Chapters 2–4), so performance levels off then too.

Since individuals do not evolve after starting work, adult organizations will also tend not to evolve. This explains why it is difficult to fundamentally improve the performance level of corporations. For example, the rate of failure of major corporate improvement programs is about 80 percent (Smith and Peters, 1996), and up to 70 percent of corporate mergers fail (Pfeffer and Sutton, 2006). Hence, also from the collective perspective in Equation 6.1 we can see why individual performance typically stagnates in the early twenties.

2. EDUCATION

Education provides theories, facts, and general skills, e.g., writing and computer skills. The theories and facts can be called "knowing what" (= understanding, German *wissen*) rather than "knowing how" (= ability to act, German *können*).

Knowledge is rewarding in itself. In addition, today's education is a necessary foundation for career directions, but does it improve general performance level? Research suggests that higher education does not affect psychological and brain development, e.g., general intelligence is remarkably stable after the age of 20 (Smith and Smith, 2005). We even found a decrease in brain integration and an increase in anxiety over a semester in college students. This lack of personal growth during higher education may be caused by education focusing on the more surface mental levels—sensory experiences, the thinking and remembering mind, and the discriminating and deciding intellect—while it does not unfold deeper mental levels. Consequently, instead of expanding and refining mind and brain, education serves more the role of filling the existing "container of knowledge."

The inability of today's education to enhance mind-brain development may explain why the extent of education has "very low validity" for predicting future job performance. The meta-analyses found that the number of years of education explained only 1 percent of overall job performance and only 4 percent of progress during training (Schmidt and Hunter, 1998, p. 272). Our matched world-class studies suggest the same conclusion: Although levels of education were similar in the world-class group and controls for each study, these two groups were consistently performing on markedly different levels. Summarizing the influence of education on performance, Schmidt and Hunter write (p. 270):

> *It is important to note that this finding does not imply that education is irrelevant to occupational success; education is clearly an important determinant of the level of job the individual can obtain. What this finding shows is that among those who apply to get a particular job, years of education does not predict future performance on that job very well. For example, for a typical semi-skilled blue-collar job, years of education among applicants might range from 9 to 12. The [very low] validity ... then means that the average job performance of those with 12 years of education will only be slightly [1 percent] higher (on average) than that for those with 9 or 10 years.*

3. PRACTICE AND WORK EXPERIENCE

Practice establishes, strengthens, refines, and modifies underlying brain circuits. Success in any demanding field of activity normally requires prolonged practice to actualize one's performance capacity. Malcolm Gladwell (2009) writes about the "10,000-Hour Rule"—for example, 3 hours per day, 6 days a week for 10 years—as a prerequisite for excelling in any field of activity. However, researchers at Princeton University recently reviewed 88 studies of deliberate practice and performance in several fields (Macnamara, Hambrick, and Oswald, 2014). Deliberate practice is defined as engagement in structured activities created specifically to improve performance in a domain. In games, the difference in performance made by practice was 26 percent; in music, 21 percent; in sports, 18 percent; in education, 4 percent; and in professional performance less than 1 percent (and not statistically significant). It thus seems that the more structured, repeatable, and predictable an activity is, the larger is the benefit of practice. This makes sense.

On average, this meta-analysis found that practice time accounted for just 12 percent of the variation in performance. Furthermore, the more rigorously each study judged its subjects' performance level, the less total practice time mattered. In one sub-sample of studies with a more rigorous assessment of performance, practice thus accounted for only 5 percent of the variance in performance.

The research at Princeton suggest that Gladwell is far too optimistic about the significance of practice. In this context, Gladwell admits, "Of course, this [10,000-Hour Rule] doesn't address why some people get more out of their practice sessions than others do" (2009, p. 44). Research has shown that "the major reason more intelligent people have higher job performance is that they acquire job knowledge more rapidly and acquire more of it" (Schmidt and Hunter, 1998, pp. 271–272). Thus, in a complex and unpredictable field, the benefits from higher mind-brain development can be expected to be larger. This increased benefit from practice through higher mind-brain development may be explained by this holistic development, bringing with it attributes such as the following:

- Greater integration of brain functioning, which is associated with higher emotional stability, more openness to experience, greater creativity, and greater problem-solving ability.

- Higher moral reasoning, which is related to a broader awareness available to make choices.

- More frequent peak experiences, which are associated with higher intrinsic motivation, autonomy, innovation, and ability to embrace feedback.

The primacy of mind-brain development may also explain why there are multi-geniuses who perform on an exceptional level in several activities, such as Michelangelo and Buckminster Fuller. Since they must have enjoyed higher personal growth, they quickly learned to master new activities.

Experience trap. Let us elaborate on the effect of practice. There is a paradox in training called the *experience trap*. Even though extensive practice may be needed to attain high performance, this does not work for everybody. In fact, continuous practice often does not lead to continuous improvement. Geoff Colvin (2010, p. 3) observes:

> *Extensive research in a wide range of fields shows that many people not only fail to become outstandingly good at what they do, no matter how many years they spend doing it, they frequently don't even get any better than they were when they started.*

The experience trap could explain why the meta-analyses cited above found that work experience has negligible influence on the general performance level—years of job experience did not correlate with progress during training, and only predicted 3 percent of overall job performance (Schmidt and Hunter, 1998).

Geoff Colvin continues that it is not practice in general that distinguishes excellence from mediocrity, but the specific type of training known as deliberate practice, which was defined above (Ericsson et al., 1993). Deliberate practice involves intrinsic motivation, intense focus and concentration, endurance (long-term perspective), and self-sufficiency (e.g., ability to train alone). These features naturally belong to higher psychological development. Thus, the effectiveness of practice may to a considerable extent depend on the level of mind-brain development, in accordance with the Unified Theory of Performance.

The common approach to performance improvement is to learn—one at a time—the various *task-specific* aspects of each profession (e.g., in management: Leadership, organizational development, accounting, economics, etc.). A complementary approach is to develop *universal* attributes by the performer directly unfolding more of his or her mind and brain. This is our focus. An example will illustrate the universal approach. Physical fitness and good mind-body coordination are universal attributes that are beneficial to all sports—yes, to life in general. Likewise, higher mind-brain development will be beneficial to any man or woman.

4. INCENTIVE PROGRAMS

It is common to use incentive programs—usually based on financial rewards—to stimulate performance, for example in business, industry, and sports. Incentives cannot increase a person's ability, only his or her effort. Thus, incentives can increase a person's performance in a simple sensorimotor task, but they do not increase performance in more complex tasks, nor do they increase the ability to think creatively or solve problems. In fact, external reinforcement generally decreases intrinsic motivation. In one study, autonomy (self-management), mastery (urge to get better), and purpose (search for meaning) were found to motivate high-level performance, whereas high bonuses decreased performance (Jensen, 2008).

Similarly, professors Alexander Cappelen and Bertil Tungodden at the business school NHH in Bergen, Norway, found that a high salary attracts persons who give first priority to earning more money for themselves rather than doing what is best for their team or corporation. In Norway, CEOs on average earn 19 times more than a normal employee; in Germany they earn 90 times more, and in the USA as much as 324 times more. Cappelen concludes that the argument that it is good to have a very high CEO salary may be a bad idea (Olsen and Skodvin, 2013).

The groundbreaking book *Punished by Rewards* by Alfie Kohn (1999) shows that while offering people incentives may in some respect work in the short run, it is a strategy that ultimately fails and even does lasting harm. Our workplaces and classrooms will continue to decline, he writes, until we begin to question our reliance on a theory of motivation derived from laboratory animals. Drawing from hundreds of studies, Kohn demonstrates that people actually do inferior work when they are enticed with money, grades, or other incentives. In the quest for high performance we therefore need to realize that as humans, we are primarily *meaning maximizers* rather than *profit maximizers*—internally driven rather than externally driven.

5. TALENT AND OTHER FACTORS WE ARE BORN WITH

Different people are born with different likes, dislikes, tendencies, and talents. Therefore, there are certain activities that are more natural for us to perform, and the easiest road to higher performance is to engage in these activities. A more developed mind and brain increasingly *enables you to recognize* what activities are most natural to you, in line with Maslow's (1968, 1971) concept of increasing self-actualization. If a donkey wishes to be the fastest animal in the world, it can practice and practice. It may become the fastest donkey in the world, but it will never beat a thoroughbred racehorse. To succeed, it is thus important to choose a profession that suits your tendencies and interests. With this, you will be able to devote full attention to your activity and not get exhausted. Rather, you will feel more energy at the end of a dynamic day than at the beginning.

Some authors argue that innate abilities or special gifts are much overrated (Coyle, 2009). The outstanding cross-country skier Thomas Alsgaard also downplays the significance of talent, and claims that the basis of his success is not inborn physical capabilities. Compared to others he does not have a bigger heart, bigger lungs, or muscles that are more enduring. In contrast, the basis of his success—even in a tough endurance sport like cross-country skiing—is the way of thinking so that one always manages to do the right thing in the right way at the right time. Notice that Thomas is describing attributes naturally belonging to higher mind-brain development. This development interacts with your specific talents in determining your level of performance. The more refined your mind and brain are, the more beneficial will this interaction be. Again, the significance of higher mind-brain development for true excellence is brought out.

Summarizing this Chapter

> *And in all of my experience, I have never seen lasting solutions to problems, [or] lasting happiness and success that came from the outside in.*
>
> — Stephen Covey (2014), American business consultant

This chapter has outlined the Unified Theory of Performance and integrated its four dimensions: Brain integration, psychological development, higher (individual) consciousness, and higher collective consciousness. We considered alternative factors that may explain excellence. Age, number of years of education, work experience, practice in activities with little routine, and incentive programs all have no or a negligible influence on performance level. The only factor that might have a significant bearing is the talent we are born with. But talent is more readily recognised and brought out with higher mind-brain development. Therefore, we conclude that mind-brain development is by far the most important factor for excellence, which means that success comes from within!

The good news is that the population in general has the potential to develop higher consciousness and thereby reach high performance. We may call this common potential the second type of talent—a *universal talent* which is much more important than any specific talent. We therefore agree with Malcolm Gladwell (2009, p. 334) when he concludes about people with exceptional performance, "Their success is not exceptional or mysterious. … The outlier, in the end, is not an outlier at all." Thus, top performers have simply expressed more of what we all have inherently as humans.

The next chapter considers activities that enhance mind-brain development and thus improve our level of performance. We will consider physical exercise, playing music, and transcendence.

Chapter 7

How to Achieve Excellence: Transform the Performer to Transform Performance

I must reassert that we have come to the point in biological history where we now are responsible for our own evolution. We have become self-evolvers.

— *Abraham Maslow (1971, p. 10)*

What is the difference between performer and performance? The performer is the person performing and his or her stage of mind-brain development is expressed in level of performance. This model means that *being* is basic to *having* and *doing*. In other words, who we are is much more important than the knowledge, skills, relationships, and resources we have, and what we do. With higher mind-brain development, our knowledge and skills become more useful, our relationships become more enriching, more resources become available, and our actions become more effective.

This chapter considers three *complementary* strategies to enhance mind-brain development and thus improve our level of performance: Physical exercise, playing music, and transcending. Transcendence appears to be the most important factor for transforming the performer.

Physical Exercise

A major study that involved 1.2 million Swedish men doing military service found that those who were physically fit at 18 had a higher IQ, were more likely to go on to university, and were more likely to secure better jobs (Åberg et al., 2009). "Being fit means that you have good heart and lung capacity and that your brain gets plenty of oxygen. This may be one of the reasons why we can see a clear link with fitness, but not with muscular strength," says Professor

Michael Nilsson at the University of Gothenburg. Maria Åberg, the main author of the study, noted:

> *We have also shown that those youngsters who improve their physical fitness between the ages of 15 and 18 increase their cognitive performance. This being the case, physical education is a subject that has an important place in schools.*

Another European study concluded that better cardiovascular fitness is associated with decreased symptoms of burnout and a better capacity to cope with stress (Gerber et al., 2013). However, if exercise by itself caused substantial mind-brain development, the world-class athletes in our research should have had the highest scores on the Performeasure assessment. Instead both the professional musicians and the top-level managers scored higher. Other researchers have made a similar observation (Shields and Bredemeier, 2001, p. 598):

> *At one time, it was widely believed that sport was valuable because it develops the character of its participants, a belief that is no longer so widely shared.*

In conclusion, physical exercise enhances physical health and mental health and happiness. However, in the bigger picture, the benefits for mind-brain development are limited.

Playing Music

Reading and math develop sequential thinking. In contrast, playing music stimulates the whole brain and enhances holistic thinking by culturing brain circuits that connect the melody with the individual notes. These circuits are important for successful decision-making and planning. As a consequence, musical training and practice during childhood leads to brain connections different than those found in typical adults today.

Two cross-sectional studies investigated the relation of music with cognitive functioning (Zuk et al., 2014). One study tested 30 adults, 15 with and 15 without musical training. The other tested 27 children, 15 with and 12 without musical training. The subjects were matched for general cognitive abilities and socioeconomic variables. All subjects were administered the Delis-Kaplan Executive Function System, a standardized battery of cognitive functioning. The most significant results that the researchers found were that children and adults who had extensive musical training showed enhanced executive function in cognitive flexibility, working memory, and processing speed. Neural imaging of the children revealed enhanced brain functioning in motor areas and frontal areas involved in emotional processing. In a third study, researchers at University of Sarasota and East Texas State University found a strong relationship between teaching music in schools and academic performance (Korsvold, 2014). These data may explain why our musicians scored higher on the Performeasure assessment than both the managers and the athletes.

Musical practice is common in society, also amongst adults. Yet research shows that in the current population, self-development and intelligence are stable during adulthood (see Chapter 3). This indicates that playing music has real but limited effects on mind-brain development.

Transcending

Transcending, either spontaneously or through meditation practices, leads to higher frontal brain blood flow and higher frontal alpha1 (8–10 Hz) EEG coherence—the frontal executive centers are functioning as a whole. Repeated experiences of transcending help to culture brain connections, leading to higher brain integration throughout the day. As we shall see later, research shows that this most fundamental experience enhances all the four dimensions of performance shown in Figure 7.1. First, repeated transcendence refines the individual level of brain integration that in turn supports higher psychological functioning and the development of higher consciousness. Second, it enhances the quality of collective consciousness. Thus, another way of formulating the Unified Theory of Performance is that the more familiar a person is with the process of transcending, the greater performance capacity he or she has. Enlivening transcendence is the main topic of this chapter.

Chapter 4 contained a number of peak experiences reported by top performers during their best performances. These moments of transcendence, expanded vision, and inner fulfillment transform one's personality. Maslow's opinion was that peak moments "can have very, very important consequences" (1971, p. 170).

Peak experiences are spontaneous and unfortunately cannot be brought about at will. The cross-country skier Thomas Alsgaard agrees: "I have been

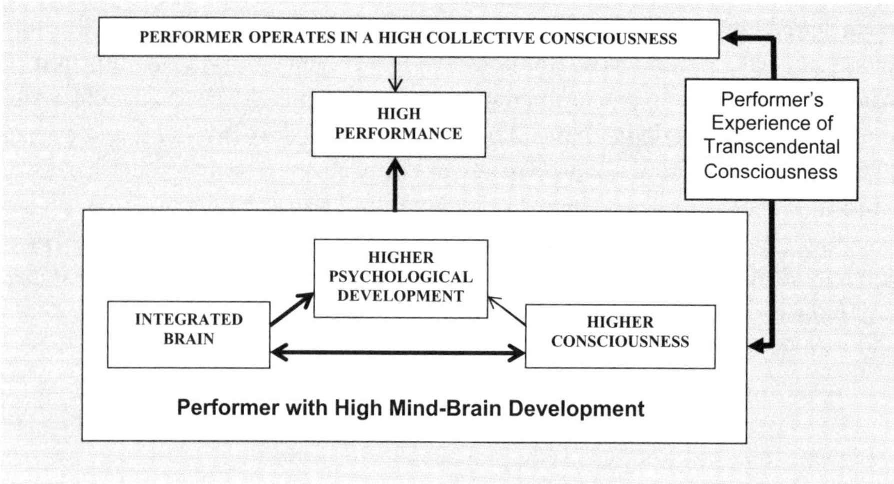

Figure 7.1 The Influence of the Experience of Transcendental Consciousness on High Performance

working on this my whole life, and it is not possible to govern this." The professional clarinet player Christian Stene noted:

> *I have this [peak] experience during certain concerts/performances. I perform at my best then and feel most creative. But I cannot force this condition to happen. Either it is happening or not. I wish that I could turn it on during all concerts, but this is unfortunately not possible. It can be described as a state of euphoria.*

The world-class golfer Tony Jacklin (Leonard, 1974, p. 43) talks about living fully in the present, not moving out of it, when performing in a peak experience, and continues:

> *It comes and it goes, and the pure fact that you are out on the first tee of a tournament and say "I must concentrate today" is no good. It won't work. It has to be already there.*

To trigger significant mind-brain growth, there need to be more frequent peak experiences and higher intensity of such experiences than what is common today. The essential question is therefore: How can we *systematically* bring about repeated peak experiences in order to facilitate mind-brain development and higher performance? In *Megatrends 2010,* Patricia Aburdene

(2007, p. xvi) writes, "The best way to cultivate consciousness is through techniques like meditation."

Meditation Practices and Transcending

All meditations explore inner consciousness, but they differ in procedures, intent, brain patterns, and effects (Orme-Johnson and Walton, 1998; Travis and Shear, 2010). Comparative research has grouped meditation practices into three fundamental categories. Table 7.1 shows the fundamentally different brain wave frequencies for these three different classes of meditation:

1. *Focused attention*. Meditations in this category focus the attention on a part of the body or an emotion. When other thoughts intrude, attention is directed back to the focus. Whenever we focus sharply we primarily see gamma brain waves (30–50 Hz; see Table 2.1), and gamma brain waves are found in meditations that involve focusing, such as Zen, Compassion meditation, or Vipassana.

2. *Open monitoring*. Meditations in this category involve dispassionate observation of the breath, bodily states, thoughts, or feelings that may arise. Theta2 (6–8 Hz) brain waves are seen when we follow internal mental processes (e.g., trying to remember something), and such brain waves are found in meditations that involve observation of inner mental processes, such as mindfulness meditation or Kriya yoga.

3. *Automatic self-transcending*. To be in this category, the meditation has to transcend its steps of practice. When the attention is awake and turned within, we see alpha1 brain waves (8–10 Hz). Alpha1 brain waves are reported during Transcendental Meditation (TM) practice. The term "automatic" is important in this category; if one uses cognitive skills such as evaluation, response selection, and attention regulation, then the mind remains active and it will not settle down and reach transcendence.

Table 7.1 The Distinctive Brain Waves of the Three Different Classes of Meditation

Focused Attention	**... voluntary focusing of attention on a chosen object (Lutz et al., 2008)**	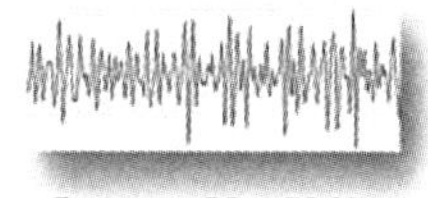 **Gamma: 30 – 50 Hz**
Open Monitoring	**... nonreactive monitoring of the content of experience from moment to moment (Lutz et al., 2008)**	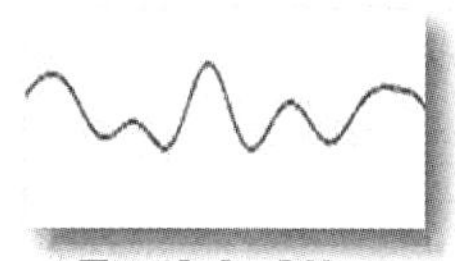 **Theta2: 6 – 8 Hz**
Automatic Self-Transcending	**... transcend the steps of the meditation practice leading to Transcendental Consciousness (Travis & Shear, 2010)**	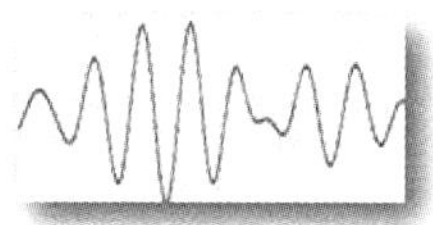 **Alpha1: 8 – 10 Hz**

Different Meditations Give Different Benefits

Different procedures during the meditation result in different effects on the performer and his or her behavior. Meditation practices in the first two categories use the thinking mind (see Table 7.1) to create cognitive strategies for coping with challenging situations after the meditation practice, such as coping with arguments or dealing with strong emotions. You are learning how to use a tool, such as learning how to use a knife.

Transcendental Meditation (TM) in the third category is not intended to develop a particular cognitive skill. Rather this technique leads to an enhancement of the mental state of the performer. Through automatic self-transcendence, TM allows the mind to reach Transcendental Consciousness—silent wakefulness underlying thoughts and feelings. Transcendence transforms how we see the world. After transcendence, your mind is sharper, clearer, and more attentive in *all* situations. In terms of the knife analogy, during TM you stop using the knife and are instead sharpening it. After TM, whatever you do, as with a sharpened knife, you will be more effective.

Since the procedures and resulting brain waves are fundamentally different in the three meditation categories, we can expect different benefits in daily life. A major meta-analysis reported larger effects of Transcendental Meditation on decreasing negative emotions, neuroticism, and anxiety, and improving self-realization, perception, behavior, and learning and memory compared to all other meditations investigated (Sedlmeier et al., 2012). In the following, we will use research on TM to illustrate the benefits that result from systematic and repeated transcendence.

The Transcendental Meditation Technique

> *The Transcendental Meditation technique is a simple, effortless way to dive within, to experience an ocean of pure consciousness, pure creativity, pure knowingness. It's a unique experience but also very familiar—it is your own Self.*
>
> — David Lynch (2014), American filmmaker

Transcendental Meditation is a simple and effortless technique without concentration, control, and belief that allows the mind to spontaneously settle down (Maharishi, [1963] 2001, 1969). It is practiced for 20 minutes twice daily sitting quietly with the eyes closed. A specific thought or mantra—utilized for its sound quality without reference to meaning—is used to facilitate the shift of attention away from the surface, active thinking level to progressively deeper or finer mental levels until even the faintest thought is completely transcended.

Since the technique involves effortless, automatic, and progressive refinement of mental activity, people quickly master transcending *during* the practice. Figure 7.2 shows that with only two months of regular transcendence, frontal brain coherence reaches its optimal level during the practice. The figure also shows that coherence remains at that high level when measured after six and twelve months of practice. However, notice that frontal coherence continues to grow in activity *after* meditation practice throughout the 12 months—this is the gradual growth of higher consciousness. Each meditation sitting is very pleasant and blissful. Yet we do not meditate for the sake of meditation; we meditate for the sake of bringing inner silence and happiness into our active life.

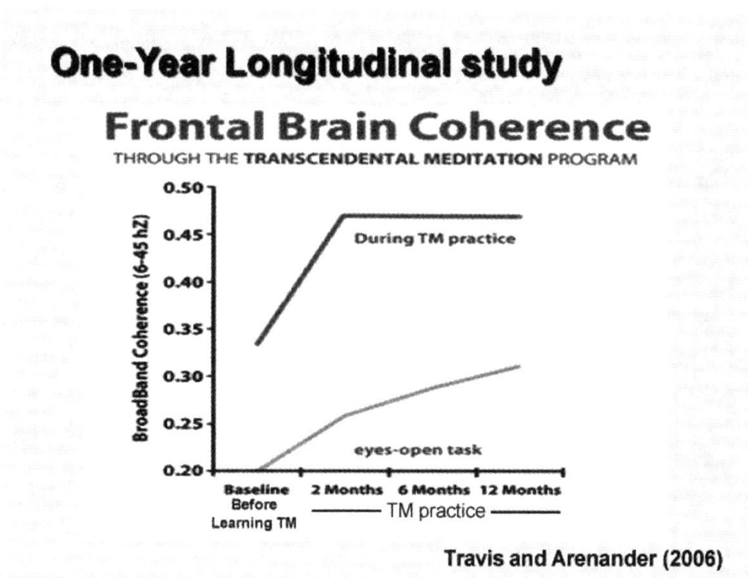

Figure 7.2 Growth of Brain Integration during TM Practice and Activity

Repeated Transcending Improves All Four Performance Dimensions

The benefits from transcending can be directly seen in each of the four performance dimensions covered in earlier chapters. First, we will consider the impact of Transcendental Consciousness on the three *individual* dimensions (including health), and how these improvements impact individual performance. Second, we will mention the impact of transcendence on *collective* consciousness and behavior.

PERFORMANCE DIMENSION 1: BRAIN INTEGRATION AND IMPROVED HEALTH

> *I've been practicing Transcendental Meditation most of my life. I think that does something to your nervous system. It has given me a calmness I don't think I had at 19.*
>
> — Jerry Seinfeld, entertainer, USA (2014)

Transcending supports growth of brain integration. Random assignment research with college students at American University in Washington, DC, reported that 10-week practice of the TM technique led to higher Brain Integration Scale scores, as shown in Figure 7.3. In contrast, the

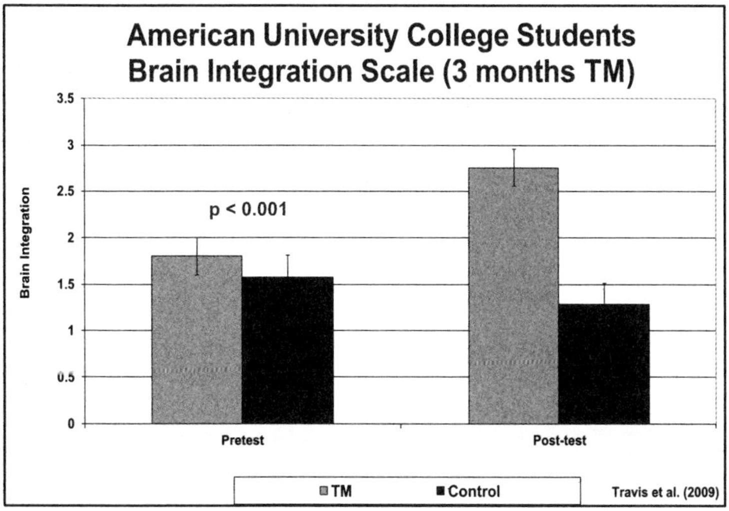

Figure 7.3 Change in Brain Integration Scale Score over 10 Weeks

non-meditating control students significantly *decreased* in brain integration during the same period. The transcending students also exhibited significantly lower anxiety and depression levels, and significantly higher behavior and coping skills. The post-test was during final examinations' week. Higher brain integration at post-test demonstrates the effect of transcending on buffering stress during a challenging period.

High brain integration is reported in world-class professionals, as discussed in Chapter 2. When the brain is more integrated, thinking and action are more powerful. Repeated transcendence thus cultures the style of brain functioning seen in highly successful people.

Figure 7.4 presents two sets of pictures of brain wave coherence in a typical adult who had been practicing the TM technique for seven years. The upper part shows coherence during an eyes-open reaction time task; the lower part shows coherence during TM practice, which is practiced with eyes closed. In each of the two pictures there are three columns of heads representing coherence in three different frequency bands—alpha, beta, and gamma (see Table 2.1). The dots on the heads are the locations of the sensors that recorded EEG. There are lines between sensor locations if the coherence between those two points is greater than 70 percent. Notice that the upper part shows that during a task there are more lines—higher coherence—in the gamma frequency band. This is what is needed to handle a challenging task.

In contrast, as shown in the lower part, there is no gamma coherence during Transcendental Consciousness. Recall that TM practice does not require concentration or control of the mind. Instead, during TM practice we find very high levels of alpha coherence—front to back and side to side—characterizing the state of transcendence and restful alertness.

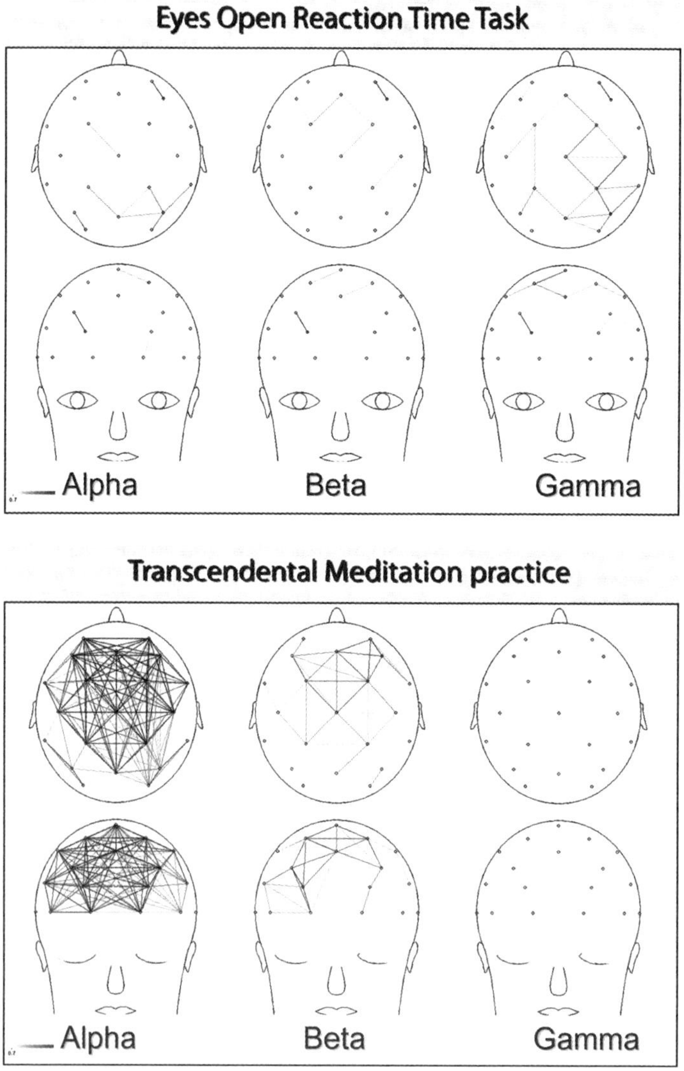

Figure 7.4 **Brain Coherence Maps during an Eyes Open Reaction Time Task (Upper Part) and During the Practice of Transcendental Meditation (Lower Part)**

Improved health. Together with enhanced brain functioning, health and vitality are physiological foundations of excellent performance. The brain and the body are intimately related. Thus, increased brain integration should improve health. Katharina Hager-Saltnes, a professional cellist we studied, describes the healthy body she experiences during optimal performance: "The body is participating, helping me to play. It is delightful to be in it!" In contrast, stress and anxiety have negative influences on health and well-being. In fact, high levels of stress are linked to over 90 percent of diseases.

Researchers at Stanford University carried out a comparative study of 146 independent investigations and found Transcendental Meditation practice about twice as effective as other meditation and relaxation techniques in reducing long-term anxiety and stress (Eppley et al., 1989).

A randomized controlled trial—conducted in collaboration with the American Heart Association—concluded that over a ten-year period, the group that had learned the TM technique were 48 percent less likely to have a heart attack or stroke or die from all causes compared with participants who attended a conventional health education class. For the subgroup that continued meditating for the whole 10-year period, the reduction was 66 percent (Schneider et al., 2012).

The National Institutes of Health (the federal medical research agency in the USA) has over a period of 20 years made available in total about USD 25 million for research on the TM technique for treatment of high blood pressure and other cardiovascular diseases. A number of universities in the USA participated in this research, which found TM practice to be as effective as medicine in reducing high blood pressure (Schneider et al., 2005). Based on a meta-analysis of the effect of a range of mental techniques, the American Heart Association concluded that the Transcendental Meditation technique is the only meditation practice that has been shown to reliably lower blood pressure (Brook et al., 2013).

An empirical study in Canada showed a 70 percent reduction in health care costs over a five-year period for a group of TM practitioners as compared to non-meditating controls (Herron et al., 1996). We can now appreciate why William Shakespeare wrote that it is the mind that makes the body rich.

PERFORMANCE DIMENSION 2: PSYCHOLOGICAL DEVELOPMENT

> *What [TM] meditation is for me is ... a moment to stop the thinking and let my heart come forward. That's how I always felt about it, because you know my thinking will drive me barmy.*
>
> — Sir Ringo Starr, formerly of The Beatles
> (Rosenthal, 2011, p. 226)

Transcending promotes psychological development. Research with children practicing the TM technique reported that transitions through Piaget's cognitive stages were smoother and faster than in non-meditating controls (Dixon et al., 2005). Higher brain integration is associated with higher levels of moral maturity, as noted earlier.

Two studies on adults found significant improvement of self-actualization. First, a ten-year investigation of ego or self-development concluded that those who practiced the TM technique increased significantly on this measure (Chandler et al., 2005). The number of meditating subjects that scored on the self-actualizing stage increased from 9 percent at pre-test to 38 percent at post-test, compared to 1 percent of control samples functioning from this level at both pre-test and post-test (about 1 percent is the norm in today's society). The meditating group achieved the highest score ever recorded on this test—including Harvard University alumni and senior management samples.

Second, a statistical meta-analysis was carried out of all existing studies (42 treatment outcomes) on the effects of the TM technique and other forms of meditation and relaxation techniques on self-actualization (Alexander et al., 1991). The improvement through TM practice was approximately *three* times as large as that of other mental techniques.

PERFORMANCE DIMENSION 3: HIGHER CONSCIOUSNESS

Repeated experience of transcendence seems to lead to growth of higher states of consciousness. Frequency of witnessing sleep increased significantly over two years in students practicing TM, while there was no significant change in non-meditating students (Cranson et al., 1991). Cross-sectional studies discussed in Chapter 4 reported brain wave patterns suggestive of Cosmic Consciousness during sleep and waking in long-term TM practitioners, while such patterns were not found in short-term TM practitioners and non-TM practitioners.

HIGH PERFORMANCE IN DIFFERENT AREAS

Regular transcendence not only improves the *basis* of higher performance, as seen above; as predicted by the Unified Theory of Performance it also improves performance *itself*.

Improvements in education. The true objective of education is to actualize full human potential. Yet in Chapter 6 we saw that this goal is not achieved today. By adding TM practice to the classroom, the objective of education is realized, as shown by many studies. Transcending students find that learning is faster and easier, that they are not affected by the stress of their education, that they are more purposeful in their lives, and that they are happier. Meditating students also have higher completion rates and are more likely to be accepted to post-secondary institutions (Colbert and Nidich, 2013).

Improvements in business. Ray Dalio is the founder and president of Bridgewater Associates, a hedge fund that he started in 1975 in his spare bedroom. Bridgewater became the largest hedge fund in the world with more than 1,000 employees. Ray has been practicing the TM technique for over 40 years, since he was a student. He comments (Rosenthal, 2011, pp. 221–223):

> *It is a combination of relaxation and a very blissful experience ... it changed the way I was thinking in two ways: It made me more centered, and also more creative. With a more centered, more open state of mind, everything got better. ... Everything became easier. ... Meditation helped my creativity. I find that creative ideas don't come from working hard, they come when I'm very relaxed, they pass through my brain, and I grab them.*
>
> *When I look back at my life, I am happy to have had what most people would consider a successful life, not only in terms of business, but in my relationships and in lots of ways. Most importantly, I have been married to the same woman for thirty-five years, and we are deeply in love. Our whole family is very close, and I have great friendships. More than anything else, I attribute it to meditation—partly because of the creativity, partly because of the centeredness.*

Subjects who learned the Transcendental Meditation technique grew significantly more than controls in their expression of leadership behaviors (McCollum, 1999). Swedish managers improved in holistic thinking and became much more perceptive of the important issues facing the company

(Gustavsson, 1992). Other benefits in business from the experience of systematic transcending include resiliency in stressful situations, new abilities to resolve conflicts, and improved job satisfaction (Alexander et al., 1993; Schmidt-Wilk, 2000, 2003).

Improvements in sports. A randomized study in sports reported significant improvements over six weeks for TM practitioners as compared to non-meditating controls for tests on running speed, agility, standing broad jump, reaction time and coordination, cardiovascular efficiency, and respiratory efficiency (Reddy et al., 1977). According to Willie Stargell, outfielder, member of the Baseball Hall of Fame, USA (World Plan Films, 1976):

> *I like TM because it helps me relax. I'm refreshed where before I wasn't. A lot of times I would wake up in the morning with nothing but a tired body to carry me through a strenuous day. I have nothing to say but pluses for it. … It might just be the key to everything.*

PERFORMANCE DIMENSION 4: RAISING THE LEVEL OF COLLECTIVE CONSCIOUSNESS

> *In moments of madness, [TM] meditation has helped me find moments of serenity. … I think meditation offers a moment in your day to be at peace with yourself and therefore the universe.*
>
> — Sir Paul McCartney, formerly of The Beatles
> (Rosenthal, 2011, p. 226)

Abraham Maslow (1998, p. 96) wrote that an increase in coherence in a person simultaneously increases the coherence of their social context. Recent research supports this prediction: The regular experience of transcendence by relatively few individuals positively affects the collective consciousness of teams, organizations, and society.

Teams and organizations. Several team benefits were found in three European top management teams who practiced TM (Schmidt-Wilk, 2000):

- Improved communication.
- Increased awareness of company and team needs and values.
- Fewer arguments.

- Move to fact-based decision-making.
- Increased mutual acceptance.
- Greater trust and openness.
- Greater happiness.
- Greater alignment.

Patricia Aburdene (2007) writes about a Detroit chemical-manufacturing company, H. A. Montgomery, which experienced dramatic benefits when 52 out of the company's 70 workers practiced the TM technique twice daily. The workers meditated 20 minutes at home before work and in the afternoon on company time at the plant. Absenteeism fell 85 percent, injuries fell 70 percent, sick days dropped 76 percent, productivity increased 120 percent, quality control rose 240 percent, and profits increased as much as 520 percent.

These large collective benefits may in part be explained by a Swedish study, which found that programs to improve the health of associates may have a double effect—the same procedures that reduce health-related absenteeism also improve the productivity of the employees. Productivity improvements, when converted into money, were about five times greater than the cost savings due to reduced health-based absenteeism (Johanson, 1999).

Society. Several studies have demonstrated that a small group of people practicing the TM and advanced TM-Sidhi programs can positively influence the quality of life of society as a whole. Improvements include reduced city crime, reduced conflicts and war intensity, and improved quality of national life (e.g., Orme-Johnson et al., 1988; Hagelin et al., 1999; Davies and Alexander, 2005). This effect of consciousness being a field (see Chapters 4 and 5) takes place when the *coherence-creating group* is as small as the square root of one percent of the population. For the USA, this means a critical group size of about 2,000 persons—for Norway 230 and for the world about 9,000. Coherence-creating groups are being established in India, USA, and several countries in Latin America.

Summarizing this Chapter

In this chapter, we discussed the importance of transforming the performer to transform performance: Enhancing the mind-brain development of the performer improves performance capacity. We examined physical exercise, playing music, and systematic transcending and found that the last factor was by far the most important for enhancing mind-brain development, including creating better health. Transcendental Consciousness is like a bath for the mind that affects all aspects of the personality and so prepares us for dynamic and successful action.

We cited research showing how the process of transcending in *one stroke* enhances all four performance dimensions in the Unified Theory of Performance, thereby providing further support of this unified theory. Hence, TM practice appears to be a key factor for developing world-class performance. Interestingly, the meditation practice itself reflects qualities of peak performance: It is enjoyable, effortless, and effective.

Chapter 8

Conclusion: Can Widespread Excellence Be Achieved?

Yoga [Transcendental Consciousness] is skill in action.
— Bhagavad Gita, ancient Vedic text (Maharishi, 1969, p. 141)

The National Olympic Training Center in Oslo is collaborating with high performers in a variety of fields to stimulate the development of future world-class performers across many areas. The center is working with the Norwegian Opera, Accenture, NTNU (Norwegian University of Science and Technology), Magnus Carlsen (world champion chess player), Ole Edvard Antonsen (world-class trumpet soloist), and Satyricon (a well-known black metal band). The idea is to establish a national high-performance culture in Norway that is common to athletes, dancers, musicians, chess players, business people, researchers, etc. This initiative largely focuses on developing mental skills, attitudes, and values. The center's CEO, Jarle Aambø, admits that this cross-disciplinary approach to excellence is breaking the normal boundaries of developing peak performance (Hansen, 2009).

This interdisciplinary, psychological approach is the first step. The second step, this book suggests, is to foster holistic mind-brain development as the basis of high performance in any profession or human activity. First, such development will improve your general performance capacity. Second, it will make it easier for you to find and express your inborn talents.

Since mind-brain development is *the* most important factor for excellence in any profession or human activity, such growth provides a truly universal basis for world-class performance. To fully realize the goal of generalized peak performance, we therefore have to extend the current paradigm to include a universal approach that integrates East and West, ancient and modern.

Universal Approach

Modern science has been instrumental in creating high performance in a wide range of material activities such as information and communication technology and space science. Even so, to achieve widespread excellence, we need to supplement Western science with ancient knowledge from the East. This book thus integrates Eastern and Western insights in a universal approach to peak performance. The importance of this synergy for high performance is increasingly being recognized. For example, the 2011 annual conference of the Academy of Management was entitled *West Meets East: Enlightening, Balancing, Transcending*. The conference invitation starts as follows:

> *In the wake of the [2008 world economic] crisis, companies from emerging economies are among the leaders in growth and innovation, and the world appears to be in a transition from "West leads East" to "West meets East." Now, more than ever, we need business professionals—academics and managers alike—who can make sense of today's global complexity and multiplicity by thinking in broad and integrative ways. China's re-emergence and the ascendance of India and other burgeoning economies offer an opportunity for revolutionary thinking based on the promise of "East-West" integrative thinking and practice.*

Simplifying a Complex Field

High performance has been considered a complicated field consisting of a number of largely independent factors, such as education, age, practice and work experience, and incentives. We have examined what research has to say about these factors, one by one: (1) Education provides important task knowledge and skills, but has practically no influence on level of performance in general. (2) In adults, age has zero effect on performance. (3) Practice and work experience may be important for skill development but are no guarantee of high performance—in fact, two major meta-analyses conclude that work experience only predicts 3 percent of overall job performance. Another meta-analysis concluded that practice explains less than 1 percent of professional performance. (4) Incentives improve performance only for simple sensorimotor tasks but have no benefits for improving performance in more complex and sophisticated professional work.

There is a growing appreciation of the value of certain mental attributes for peak performance, even in physically demanding endurance sports: Attributes such as finding win-win solutions, a long-term and holistic perspective, growth-orientation, pro-action instead of reaction, self-reliance, effortless performance, joy, and spontaneous right action. It is thought that through hard work and determination individuals can learn these mental qualities. However, as this book documents, the required attributes of excellence are largely *not learned* but are instead qualities that *spontaneously* unfold with higher mind-brain development.

We saw that exercise is beneficial for physical and mental health and well-being and that playing music leads to some improvements of mind and brain. Yet both exercise and music seem only to cause limited mind-brain development. Education, practice, and work experience activate isolated brain areas and circuits only, without promoting an integrated functioning of the whole brain. The fundamental reason why these common activities aimed at enhancing performance have a limited impact is that they do not markedly refine psychology and physiology. Therefore, transforming mind and brain is in itself by far the most important strategy for achieving excellence, in accordance with our Unified Theory of Performance. In other words, mind-brain development is *the* "active ingredient" in performance.

Transcendence is Key

How can we achieve mind-brain development in practice? So far education and practice have focused on the body, senses, and more surface mental levels to improve performance. This book shows that deeper mental levels, in particular the experience of Transcendental Consciousness, are the key to lasting and generalized top performance. The challenge is that the deeper mental levels normally are *hidden*, beyond our conscious reach. We have presented research showing that these fundamental levels can be unfolded in practice through the simple and effortless technique of Transcendental Meditation, which is based on the principle "no pain, maximum gain." We could also say, "more joy, more gain." Identifying an expanded awareness as the basis of increasing effectiveness of thinking and behavior gives a new foundation for excellence.

Mind-brain development has four dimensions: Brain integration, psychological development, higher consciousness, and the level of the collective consciousness in which the performer operates. The key to the experience of transcendence is the brain, which is dynamically shaped by natural maturation and ongoing life experience—experiences ranging from stressful to the bliss of the transcendent. Over time, frequent experiences of Transcendental Consciousness naturally result in higher consciousness, characterized by restful alertness, playfulness, and peak performance. Table 8.1 presents a list of qualities that top performers report in this book during optimal performance. These beautiful qualities spontaneously flower as higher consciousness dawns and facilitates higher performance for all of us.

The few people in post-conventional development may explain why so far there has only been limited progress in many fields of life, such as ethics, empathy, social rehabilitation, and performance in general. Despite millions of books and articles, major problems continue in the world.

Table 8.1 Attributes of World-class Performance in Higher Consciousness

<table>
<tr>
<td>• Absorption
• Action in accordance with natural law
• Acting on gut feeling and instinct
• Alertness
• Automation in action
• Beauty
• Being in control
• Being in the right place at the right time
• Beyond time
• Bliss
• Body moves naturally
• Coherence
• Delightful
• Do less and accomplish more
• Economical action
• Ecstasy
• Effortlessness
• Endurance
• Energy
• Eternity
• Euphoria
• Everything is right
• Excellence
• Exhilaration</td>
<td>• Expanded awareness
• Focus
• Fulfillment
• Good fortune
• Happiness
• Harmony
• Ignoring distractions
• Improved time management
• Inner calmness amidst outer dynamic activity
• Intrinsic motivation
• Intuition
• Invincibility
• Joy
• Knowing oneself
• Least action
• Liberation
• Luck
• Mind-body coordination
• No friction, resistance, or obstacles
• No negative thoughts
• No strain, maximum gain
• No stress
• Nourishing</td>
<td>• Peaceful
• Perfection
• Playfulness
• Powerful
• Restful alertness
• Rich and refined perception
• Right timing
• Self
• Self-referral
• Self-sufficiency
• Simplicity
• Spontaneous right action
• Successful
• Tranquility
• Transcendence
• Transcending ordinary space and time
• Tunnel combined with greatly expanded awareness
• Unity with others and the surroundings
• Wakefulness
• Wholeness
• Witnessing</td>
</tr>
</table>

Many Global Improvements Taking Place

> *I hold that mankind is approaching an era in which peace treaties will not only be recorded on paper, but will also become inscribed in the hearts of men.*
>
> — Albert Einstein (Martin and Ott, 2013, p. viii)

Fortunately, there are also many signs of a global change for the better, indicating that the collective consciousness of the world is on the rise. The level of intelligence has risen by 43 percent during the last 100 years (Flynn, 2012). According to UNICEF, infant mortality has been halved during the last 20 years. According to the well-known economist Jeffrey D. Sacks (2015), the world has made major progress in eliminating extreme poverty. From 1990 to January 2015, he estimates that the percentage of people living in extreme poverty has declined from 43 percent to around 15 percent.

Narrow national patriotism is being transcended, especially by the young through the use of the Internet. The quest for sustainability is also contributing to a more unified world. Never before has the level of wealth been so high, and the standard of living is increasing. There is also a continued increase in the level of education. Human lifespan is increasing and is related to improved diet and increased height—for every centimeter a person is taller, life expectancy increases by 1.2 years (OECD, 2014). Peace research institutes tell us that never before in known history has the world been more peaceful than now. And the interest in higher consciousness is growing day by day.

A study of 40,000 secondary school students in Norway found that (1) 19 out of 20 enjoy going to school, (2) they are happy with their parents, don't smoke, drink less alcohol, and exercise at least once a week, and (3) three out of four think they are going to have a happy life (NOVA, 2013).

The need to grow and progress is fundamental to life. We take it for granted that material comfort will increase, that computers will become faster and more sophisticated, that the value of the stock market will continue to rise, and that records in sports will be broken. In many ways this urge for *outer* development is at the basis of the sustainability problem. Nations simply cannot reach agreement on limiting, for example, CO_2 emission because it is thought that such limits may restrict material growth. In addition, to some extent the present environmental concerns may be related to the prominence of object-referral in people's reality – we are depending too much on the environment for our sense of security and well-being.

The widespread awakening of *inner* development will solve these problems. First, it is the only way to permanently satisfy the never-ending human quest for progress, since there appear to be no limits to mind-brain development. Second, it creates no pollution; in contrast, it spreads harmony in the surroundings. Third, it enhances self-referral happiness, self-confidence, creativity, and empathy and creates a post-conventional reality, which should increasingly enable us to solve environmental and other problems. Thus, we can appreciate Maharishi Mahesh Yogi ([1963] 2001) when he says that the goal of life is 200 percent: 100 percent of inner growth of higher consciousness and 100 percent of outer growth of material comfort.

Everyone Wants Excellence and Happiness

Every individual wants excellence and happiness. Since transcendence—the key to happiness, good health, and world-class performance—is *the* most fundamental mental level in *every* human being, this suggests that widespread excellence and happiness should be possible. With the global unfolding of higher mind-brain development we thus foresee a brighter future for the world—a world characterized by joy, harmony, peace, and progress (Maharishi, 1976b). In such a golden age the focus will naturally shift from the current reactive attention to problems to a proactive and solution-based approach and an accelerated development of full human potential. On this platform, we expect that true peak performance soon will be not the exception but the norm.

Appendix 1: Definition of Important Terms

Achiever	Person operating at the upper end of the conventional range of ego or self-development
Alignment in Organizations	Members of an organization working together in accordance with organizational goals, core purpose, and core values; coherence in organizations
Alpha1 Brain Waves (8–10 Hz)	Associated with wakefulness, restful alertness, transcendence, higher brain blood flow
Alpha2 Brain Waves (10–13 Hz)	Associated with idling; brain modules are primed to be used, but are inactive. Brain blood flow is lower than for alpha1 brain waves
Amygdala	Part of the brain that adds emotional significance to memory and experience
Basal Ganglia	Part of the brain associated with muscle memory
Beta1 Brain Waves (16–20 Hz)	Associated with ongoing processing of experience

Beta2 Brain Waves (20–30 Hz)	Associated with focus or concentration
Brain Stem	"Lower" brain structures
Broadband Coherence	Brain wave coherence across a wide range of frequencies—6–40 Hz
CEO of the Brain	Prefrontal cortex, the executive center of the brain
Cerebral Cortex (or simply Cortex)	Brain's outer layer
Cognition	Mental processes of the thinking mind and the deciding intellect
Coherence-creating Group	A small group of people practicing the TM and TM-Sidhi program together and thereby spreading harmony throughout society
Coherence in Brain Functioning	Brain waves from different parts of the brain have a stable relationship. Coherence between two different brain areas suggests those areas are working together
Collective Consciousness	Overall consciousness of a collection of individuals such as a family, team, organization, city, nation, or the world. It is a direct and sensitive reflection of the level of consciousness of its individual members, their stage of mind-brain development

Consciousness	Ranges from individual conscious experience to a fundamental field of wakefulness underlying nature (pure consciousness)
Consciousness, Development of	Mind-brain development
Corporate Culture	Shared values, attitudes, and ways of doing things in an organization
Cortex	Brain's outer layer
Cosmic Consciousness	Transcendental Consciousness coexisting with waking, sleeping, and dreaming. Perception is the same as during the normal waking state, i.e., perception is limited to the surface levels of the object
Delta Brain Waves (1–4 Hz)	Most common during the deepest periods of sleep when the brain is being repaired
Development of Consciousness	Mind-brain development
EEG	Electroencephalography: Using electrodes fastened to the scalp to measure electrical brain wave activity
Ego	Core of the individual that integrates all mental levels into meaningful experiences; the "experiencer"

Egocentric	Narrow selfishness and low levels of empathy and moral reasoning
Ego Development in Psychology	Growth in how we view ourselves, others, and the world to make meaning of our lives
Ego-integration	Highest developmental stage in modern psychology at the upper end of the post-conventional range. It represents fullest unfolding of individual ego; also called self-realization
Ego-transcendence	Transcendental Consciousness
Electroencephalography (EEG)	Using electrodes fastened to the scalp to measure electrical brain wave activity
Executive Functioning	Mental functioning that includes inhibition, problem solving, goal-directed behavior, cognitive flexibility, and maintenance of information in working memory
Extrinsic Motivation	Motivated by *outer* factors such as money, power, winning, and fame
Feelings or Feeling Level	Stable refined emotions that seek to unify and harmonize differences and that assist the intellect in discrimination and decision-making

Field	A non-local pervasive wholeness that underlies and influences the objects within its range
Flow	Performance characterized by a matching of challenge and ability
Gamma Brain Waves (30–50 Hz)	Associated with strong focus or concentration
General Intelligence	A common factor in different intelligence tests that reflects the ability to reason, plan, solve problems, think abstractly, understand complex ideas, learn quickly, make use of experience, etc.
Habituation Time	Time needed to stop reacting to irrelevant distractions, for example repeated loud sounds
Higher Consciousness	Transcendental Consciousness, Cosmic Consciousness, Refined Cosmic Consciousness, and Unity Consciousness
Higher Development	Development beyond what is normal today, i.e., unfolding feelings, ego, and Transcendental Consciousness
Higher Self	Transcendental Consciousness
Higher States of Consciousness	Higher consciousness
Hz (Hertz)	Cycles per second of a wave

Intrinsic Motivation	Motivated by *inner* happiness, autonomy, mastery, meaning, and purpose
Law of Least Action	Principle from physics of accomplishing the goal with minimal expenditure of time and energy
Limbic System	Part of the brain that controls our emotions
Lower self	Thinking mind, deciding intellect, feelings, and individual ego
Maharishi Mahesh Yogi	Founder of the Transcendental Meditation technique and the TM-Sidhi program. World-leading expert in the full range of human development
Maharishi Vedic Science	Maharishi's revitalization of the ancient Vedic tradition of knowledge from India that explores consciousness in the framework of modern science. This body of knowledge includes systematic investigation of both the inner subject and outer objects
Mental Levels	Behavior, senses, desires, mind (thinking), intellect (deciding), feelings, ego, and Transcendental Consciousness
Meta-analysis	An analysis that summarizes several research projects

Mind	Has two meanings in this book: (1) the wholeness that includes *all* mental levels, and (2) the specific mental level that performs concrete thinking, memory, and associations. In this book, it will be apparent from the context which meaning is appropriate
Mind-brain Development	Brain refinement, psychological development, and growth of higher consciousness
Myelin	Fatty layers around the neuron's axons that greatly increase the speed of propagating electrical impulses in the brain
Natural Laws	The laws governing the creation and evolution of the universe and life, as discovered by physics, chemistry, biology, etc.
Neuroplasticity	The capacity of neurons in the brain to change their patterns of connections throughout life. Also known as neural plasticity
Object-referral Happiness	The result of satisfying some specific need or desire, i.e., buying a new car
Organizational Culture	Shared values, attitudes, and ways of doing things that are found in any organization

Orienteering	A sport involving running and navigating using a map and compass in a forest; involves fully both mind and body
Peak Experience	Appears to be a glimpse of any of the four higher states of consciousness
Peak Performance	Excellent level of performance in any type of activity—also known as world-class performance
Performeasure	Assessment of mind-brain development and performance capacity. The three components are brain integration, moral reasoning, and frequency of peak experiences
Plateau Experience	Appears to be a more lasting experience of Cosmic Consciousness, Refined Cosmic Consciousness, or Unity Consciousness
Post-conventional	Advanced range of psychological development where the individual enjoys extensive freedom of thought, i.e., independent of conventional thinking
Post-conventional Experience	Gratifying inner experience related to the post-conventional range of psychological development. Acting while consciously aware of the deep mental

	levels of feelings and ego. Post-conventional experiences are precursors to peak experiences. Some authors seem to include post-conventional experiences in peak experiences
Pre-conventional	Thinking only of oneself, irrespective of norms and the collective mentality in society
Prefrontal Cortex of Brain	The frontal brain area behind the forehead that is responsible for attention, sense of self, short-term memory, planning, strategizing, decision-making, and execution; CEO of the brain
Psychological Development	Unfolding all mental levels down to individual ego, but not including Transcendental Consciousness
Pure Consciousness	Consciousness underlying all life. Pure consciousness is being investigated in modern physics as the unified field of natural law. During Transcendental Consciousness we contact pure consciousness
Refined Cosmic Consciousness	Transcendental Consciousness coexisting with the finest level of perception of the object. The surface level of the object is still perceived, but its refined value shines through as well
Self	Higher Self or Transcendental Consciousness

self	Lower self: mind, intellect, feelings, and ego
self-actualization	Highest developmental stage in modern psychology, fullest unfolding of individual ego; also called ego-integration
self-development	Ego development
self-referral happiness	Inner happiness independent of objects. The Vedic texts relate self-referral happiness or bliss to the experience of Transcendental Consciousness
Serotonin	Biochemical associated with self-esteem
Sigma Brain Waves (13–16 Hz)	Sleep onset
Strategist	A person operating in the lower part of the post-conventional range of ego or self-development
Stroop Test	A measure of reaction time when naming color words written in an ink different than the color word itself—such as the word "red" written in blue ink
Subcortical Brain	Inner brain areas responsible for arousal and reflexive responses
Survey of Peak Experiences	Questionnaire used to bring out a person's frequency of peak experiences during

	relaxation, activity, and sleep plus frequency of luck
Theta1 Brain Waves (4–6 Hz)	Dreaming and drowsiness
Theta2 Brain Waves (6–8 Hz)	Inner mental processes such as during a memory task
TM	Transcendental Meditation
TM-Sidhi	Advanced techniques of the TM program
Transcendence	Transcendental Consciousness
Transcendental Consciousness	Most fundamental mental level, most expanded depth and breadth of self-awareness, restful alertness—inner silence without thoughts, higher Self
Transcendental Meditation	Simple and effortless mental technique for settling down the mind and reaching Transcendental Consciousness
Tunnel	The performer is able to focus only on factors relevant to his or her performance; all irrelevant input is excluded. Often related to high performance
Unified Field of Natural Law	Glimpsed by modern quantum field theory in physics as the source of the universe
Unified Theory of Collective Performance	Higher collective consciousness forms the basis of higher collective performance in any organization or society

Unified Theory of Leadership	Higher mind-brain development provides the basis of more effective leadership in any profession or field of activity
Unified Theory of Performance	Higher mind-brain development provides the basis of higher individual performance in any profession or field of activity
Unity Consciousness	Experiencing everything—inner and outer—in terms of the Self. Highest level of human development
Veda	Veda means knowledge, both subjective and objective. Veda is among the oldest continuing traditions of knowledge in the world. It provides a comprehensive description of the full range of human development
Witnessing	Simultaneous experience of inner silence of Transcendental Consciousness with waking, sleeping, and dreaming

Appendix 2: Names of World-class Performers

This appendix deals with the names of the performers in our four world-class performance studies.

Study 1. World-class Performers in a Variety of Professions

The names of all 40 peak performers, who came from 16 different countries, are presented by Harung (1999).

Study 2. World-class Athletes

The following Norwegian high-performing athletes, who are quoted in this book, have agreed to having their names disclosed:

Thomas Alsgaard	Male cross-country skier who won 11 gold medals in Olympic Games or world championships. At the ages of 40 and 41 Thomas made a comeback and both years finished third in the Norwegian championship 15 km cross-country skiing race
Susann Goksør Bjerkrheim	Female handball player who was part of the national team winning one gold, one silver, and one bronze in world championships, two silver and one bronze in Olympic Games, and one silver and one bronze in European championships

Bjørn Rune Gjelsten	Male offshore boat racer who won a record five Class 1 powerboat World Cups. He is also a highly successful businessman
Trude Dybendahl Hartz	Female cross-country skier who won one gold, three silver, and two bronze medals in world championships, and three silver medals in Olympic Games
Ingrid Kristiansen	Female long-distance runner who set six world records from 5000m on track to marathon. Her marathon world record held for 13 years. She is the only runner in the world who held world records in 5000m, 10000m, half-marathon, and marathon at the same time
Hege Riise	Female soccer player who was part of the national team winning one world championship, one Olympic Games championship, and one European championship
Hanne Staff	Female orienteer who won four world championships and two World Cups
Heidi Tjugum	Female handball goalkeeper who was part of the team that won one world championship, one European championship, two European cups, and a number of silver and bronze medals in such championships
Bjørnar Valstad	Male orienteer who won four world championships and one World Cup

Study 3. Top-level Managers

The top-level managers quoted are anonymous.

Study 4. Professional Classical Musicians

For most of the professional classical musicians, the name is given when they are quoted in the text; a few musicians chose to remain anonymous.

References

Åberg, M. A. I., Pedersen, N. L., Torén, K., Svartengren, M., Bäckstrand, B., Johnsson, T., Cooper-Kuhn, C. M., Åberg, N. D., Nilsson, M. and Kuhn, H. G. (2009). Cardiovascular fitness is associated with cognition in young adulthood. *Proceedings of the National Academy of Sciences (PNAS)*, 106(49), 20906–20911.

Aburdene, P. (2007). *Megatrends 2010: The Rise of Conscious Capitalism*. Hampton Roads Publishing Company, Charlottesville, Virginia, USA.

Alexander, C. and Boyer, R. W. (1989). Seven states of consciousness: Unfolding the full potential of the cosmic psyche in individual life through Maharishi Vedic Psychology. *Modern Science and Vedic Science*, 2(4), 358.

Alexander, C., Davies, J., Dixon, C. A., Dillbeck, M., Druker, S., Oetzel, R. M., Muehlman, J. M. and Orme-Johnson, D. (1990). Growth of higher stages of consciousness: Maharishi Vedic Psychology of human development. In Alexander, C. N. and Langer, E. (eds), *Higher Stages of Human Development*. Oxford University Press, New York, USA, 259–341.

Alexander, C. N., Rainforth, M. V. and Gelderloos, P. (1991). Transcendental Meditation, self-actualization, and psychological health: A conceptual overview and statistical meta-analysis. *Journal of Social Behavior and Personality*, 6(5), 189–247.

Alexander, C. N., Swanson, G. C., Rainforth, M. V., Carlisle, T. W., Todd, C. C. and Oates, R. M. (1993). Effects of the Transcendental Meditation program on stress reduction, health, and employee development: A prospective study in two occupational settings. *Anxiety, Stress and Coping: An International Journal*, 6, 245–262.

Alsgaard, T. (2008). *Best på ski* (Best on skis). Tun Forlag, Oslo, Norway, 142–153.

Antzoulatos, E. G. and Miller, E. K. (2014). Increases in functional connectivity between prefrontal cortex and striatum during category learning. *Neuron*. Available online 12 June.

Argument Gruppen. (2003). *Topplederundersøkelse om Corporate Social Responsibility* (Top-level Manager Survey on CSR), Argument Gruppen AS, March, Oslo, Norway, www.argument.no.

Argyle, M. (2001). *The Psychology of Happiness*. Routledge, Brighton, England.

Aristotle. (1998). *Nikomachische Ethik*, Frankfurt am Main, Germany.

Arnold, D. F. and Ponemon, L. A. (1991). Internal auditors' perceptions of whistle-blowing and the influence of moral reasoning: An experiment. *Auditing: A Journal of Practice & Theory*, 10 (Fall), 1–15.

Arnulf, J. K. (2009). www.journalisten.no, 4 December.

Atkins, C. (2013). http://bleacherreport.com/articles/1604854-how-much-does-home-field-advantage-matter-in-soccer, 15 April.

Bannister, R. (2004). *The Four-Minute Mile*. The Lyons Press/Globe Pequot Press, Guilford, Connecticut, USA.

Baumeister, R. F. and Tierney, J. (2011). *Willpower: Rediscovering the Greatest Human Strength*. Penguin Press, New York, USA.

Benedek, M., Bergner, S., Konen, T., Fink, A. and Neubauer, A. C. (2011). EEG alpha synchronization is related to top-down processing in convergent and divergent thinking. *Neuropsychologia*, 49(12), 3505–3511.

Blank, W. (1995). *The 9 Natural Laws of Leadership*. American Management Association, New York, USA.

Bloomberg.com (2011). The 50 most innovative companies 2010. Boston Consulting Group, *Business Week* and *Bloomberg*. 18 July.

Boes, R., Harung, H. S., Travis, F. and Pensgaard, A. M. (2014). Mental and physical attributes defining world-class Norwegian athletes: Content analysis of interviews. *Scandinavian Journal of Medicine and Science in Sports*, 24, 422–427.

Brook, R. D., et al. (2013). Beyond medications and diet: Alternative approaches to lowering blood pressure. A scientific statement from the American Heart Association. *Hypertension*, 61, 1360–1383.

Brundtland Commission. (1987). United Nations, March 20.

Buonomano, D. V. and Merzenich, M. M. (1998). Cortical plasticity: From synapses to maps. *Annual Review of Neuroscience*, 21, 149–186.

Campbell, J. (1949). *Hero with a Thousand Faces*. Pantheon Books, Bollingen Series, New York, USA.

Caruth, D. L., Caruth, G. D. and Pane, S. S. (2009). *Staffing the Contemporary Organization: A Guide to Planning, Recruiting, and Selecting for Human Resource Professionals* (3rd ed.). Praeger, Westport, Connecticut, USA.

Chandler, H. M., Alexander, C. N. and Heaton, D. P. (2005). Transcendental Meditation and post-conventional self-development: A 10-year longitudinal study. *Journal of Social Behavior and Personality*, 17, 93–122.

Coe, S. and Miller, D. (1981). *Running Free*. Sidgwick & Jackson, London, England.

Cohn, L. D. (1998). Age trends in personality development: A quantitative review. In Westenberg, P. M., Blasi, A. and Cohn, L. D. (eds), *Personality Development: Theoretical, Empirical and Clinical Investigations of Loevinger's Conception of Ego Development*. Lawrence Erlbaum Associates, Mahwah, New Jersey, 133–143.

Colbert, R. D. and Nidich, S. (2013). Effect of the Transcendental Meditation program on graduation, college acceptance and dropout rates for students attending an urban public high school. *Education*, 133(4), 495–501.

Collins, J. C. and Porras, J. I. (2002). *Built to Last: Successful Habits of Visionary Companies*. Harper Business Essentials, New York, USA.

Colvin, G. (2010). *Talent is Overrated: What Really Separates World-class Performers from Everyone Else*. Penguin Books Ltd., London, England.

Cook-Greuter, S. (1999/2000). Post autonomous ego development: Its nature and measurement. Doctoral dissertation. Harvard Graduate School of Education. Cambridge, Massachusetts, USA. Published by UMI #9933122.

Cook-Greuter, S. (2000). Mature ego development: A gateway to ego transcendence? *Journal of Adult Development*, 7(4), 227–240.

Covey, S. D. (1989). *The 7 Habits of Highly Effective People*. Simon and Schuster, New York, USA.

Covey, S. D. (2009). Lecture at the Sondheim Center, Fairfield, Iowa, USA, 20 November.

Covey, S. D. (2014). www.wisdomatwork.com/programs/mind-fitness, as per 22 October.

Coyle, D. (2009). *The Talent Code: Greatness isn't Born. It's Grown. Here's How.* Bantam Dell, New York, USA.

Cranson, R. W., Orme-Johnson, D. W., Dillbeck, M. C., Jones, C. H., Alexander, C. N. and Gackenbach, J. (1991). Transcendental Meditation and improved performance on intelligence-related measures: A longitudinal study. *Journal of Personality and Individual Differences*, 12(10), 1105–1116.

Csíkszentmihályi, M. (1975). *Beyond Boredom and Anxiety*. Jossey Bass, San Francisco, USA.

Csíkszentmihályi, M. (1991). *Flow: The Psychology of Optimal Experience*. Harper, New York, USA.

Dam, L. (2006). *Corporate Social Responsibility and the Financial Performance Paradox*. University of Groningen, Department of Economics, the Netherlands.

Damon, W. (2004). *The Moral Advantage*. Berrett-Koehler, San Francisco, USA.

Davies, J. L. and Alexander, C. N. (2005). Alleviating political violence through reducing collective tension: Impact assessment analysis of the Lebanon war. *Journal of Social Behavior and Personality*, 17, 285–338.

Diener, E, (1985). Happiness of the very wealthy. *Social Indicators Research*, 16, 263–274.

Dillbeck, M. C. and Orme-Johnson, D. W. (1987). Physiological differences between Transcendental Meditation and rest. *American Psychologist*, 42(9), 879–881.

Dixon, C., Dillbeck, M. C., Travis, F., Msemaje, H., Clayborne, B. M., Dillbeck, S. L. and Alexander, C. H. (2005). Accelerating cognitive and self-development: Longitudinal studies with preschool and elementary school children. *Journal of Social Behavior and Personality*, 17, 65–91.

Duman, R., Heninger, G. and Nestler, E. (1997). A molecular and cellular theory of depression. *Archives of General Psychiatry*, 54, 597–606.

Eccles, R. G., Ioannou, I. and Serafeim, G. (2011). The impact of a corporate culture of sustainability on corporate behavior and performance. HBS working paper 12-035, 25 November.

Eddington, A. (1974). *The Nature of the Physical World*. The University of Michigan Press, Ann Arbor, Michigan, USA.

Einstein, A. (2014). http://quotationsbook.com/quote/38717/, 19 November.

el-Sadat, A. (1979). *In Search of Identity*. Harper & Row, New York, USA.

Emerson, R. W. (2014). www.wisdomportal.com/Emerson/Emerson-Anthology.html, as per 18 October.

Eppley, K., Abrams, A. and Shear, J. (1989). The differential effects of relaxation techniques on trait anxiety: A meta-analysis. *Journal of Clinical Psychology*, 45(6), 957–974.

Ericsson, K. A., Krampe, R. T. and Tesch-Römer, C. (1993). The role of deliberate practice in the acquisition of expert performance. *Psychological Review*, 100(3), 363–406.

Evensen, M. S. (2009a). *Like barn skaper best* (Like children are best at creating). *Aftenposten*, Jobb. Oslo, Norway, 25 January, p. 7.

Evensen, M. S. (2009b). *Har kuttet bort 19 tonn avfall i lunsjen* (Have eliminated 19 tons of waste during lunch). *Aftenposten*, Oslo, Norway, 17 February.

Ferguson, A. (2013). *My Autobiography*. Hodder & Stoughton, London, England.

Fields, R. D. and Stevens-Graham, B. (2002). New insights into neuron-glia communication. *Science*, 298(5593), 556–562.

Flynn, J. R. (2012). *Are We Getting Smarter?* Cambridge University Press, Cambridge, England.

Friedman, M. (2003). Interview in *Financial Times*, London, 7 June.

Galinsky, A., Ronay, R., Greenaway, K. and Anicich, E. M. (2012). The path to glory is paved with hierarchy: When hierarchical differentiation increases group effectiveness. *Psychological Science*, 23, 669–677.

Gallup World Poll. (2010). The World's Happiest Countries, www.forbes.com/2010/07/14/world-happiest-countries, 14 July.

Garfield, C. A. (1984). *Peak Performance: Mental Training Techniques of the World's Greatest Athletes*. Warner Books, New York, USA.

Gerber, M., Lindwall, M., Lindegård, A., Börjesson, M. and Jonsdottird, I. H. (2013). Cardiorespiratory fitness protects against stress-related symptoms of burnout and depression. *Health Promotion. Patient Education and Counseling*, 93, 146–152.

Gibbs, J. C., Arnold, K. D., Morgan, R. L., Schwarts, E. S., Gavaghan, M. P. and Tappan, M. B. (1990). Construction and validation of a measure of moral reasoning. *Child Development*, 55(2), 527–553.

Gladwell, M. (2009). *Outliers—the Story of Success*. Penguin Books Ltd., London, England.

Gottfredson, L. (1997). Why g matters: The complexity of everyday life. *Intelligence*, 24(1), 79–132.

Gotvassli, K-Å. and Haugset, A. S. (2010). Job engagement: Antecedents and effects on job performance. *Academy of Management Journal*, 53(3), 617–635.

Gustavsson, B. (1992). The transcendent organization. Unpublished doctoral dissertation, University of Stockholm, Sweden.

Hagelin, J. S. (1987). Is consciousness the unified field? A field theorist's perspective. *Modern Science and Vedic Science*, 1(1), 29–88.

Hagelin, J. S., Orme-Johnson, D. W., Rainforth, M., Cavanaugh, K. and Alexander, C. N. (1999). Results of the National Demonstration Project to Reduce Violent Crime and Improve Governmental Effectiveness in Washington, D.C. *Social Indicators Research*, 47, 153–201.

Hagelin, H. S. (2012). Foundations of physics and consciousness. Compendium for Physics 110, Maharishi University of Management, Fairfield, Iowa, USA.

Haier, R. J. (1993). Cerebral glucose metabolism and intelligence. In Vernon, P. A. (ed.), *Biological Approaches to the Study of Human Intelligence*. Ablex Publishing, New York, USA.

Hansen, E. (2009). *Skal spille sammen* (Will be playing together). *Aftenposten*, Oslo, Norway, 27 December, p. 28.

Harung, H. S., Alexander, C. N. and Heaton, D. P. (1995). A unified theory of leadership: Experiences of higher states of consciousness in world-class leaders. *Leadership and Organization Development Journal*, 16(7), 44–59.

Harung, H. S., Heaton, D. P., Graff, W. W. and Alexander, C. N. (1996). Peak performance and higher states of consciousness: A study of world-class performers. *Journal of Managerial Psychology*, 11(4), 3–23.

Harung, H. S., Alexander, C. N. and Heaton, D. P. (1999). Evolution of organizations in the new millennium. *Leadership and Organization Development Journal*, 20(3), 198–206.

Harung, H. S. (1999). *Invincible Leadership: Building Peak Performance Organizations by Harnessing the Unlimited Power of Consciousness*. M.U.M. Press, Fairfield, Iowa, USA.

Harung, H., Travis, F., Pensgaard, A. M., Boes, R., Cook-Greuter, S. and Daley, K. (2011). Higher psycho-physiological refinement in world-class Norwegian athletes: Brain measures of performance capacity. *Scandinavian Journal of Medicine and Science in Sports*, 21(1), 32–41.

Harung, H. S. (2012). Illustrations of peak experiences during optimal performance in world-class performers: Integrating Eastern and Western insights. *Journal of Human Values*, 18(1), 33–52.

Harung, H. S. and Travis, F. (2012). Higher mind-brain development in successful leaders: Testing a unified theory of performance. *Cognitive Processing*, 13(2), 171–181.

Haugli, K. B. M. (2010). *Medaljer betyr ingenting* (Medals don't mean anything). *Aftenposten*, Oslo, Norway, 19 February.

Haugli, K. B. M. (2014). *Han har tatt skiskytingen til et nytt nivå* (He has taken biathlon to a new level). *Aftenposten*, Oslo, Norway, 20 February.

Henmo, O. (2009). *Over 180 i IQ* (Above 180 in IQ). *Aftenposten*, A-Magasinet, Oslo, Norway, 16 October.

Herron, R. E., Hillis, S. L., Mandarino, J. V., Orme-Johnson, D. W. and Walton, K. G. (1996). The impact of the Transcendental Meditation program on government payments to physicians in Quebec. *American Journal of Health Promotion*, 10(3), 208–216.

Hersey, P. and Blanchard, K. H. (1969). *Management of Organizational Behavior – Utilizing Human Resources*. Prentice Hall, New Jersey, USA.

Hole, A. (2009). *Ikke vemodig, men litt rart* (Not sad, but a little strange). *Aftenposten*, Oslo, Norway, 7 March, p. 28.

Hole, A. (2013). *Slik kommer hun i kampmodus* (This is how she gets into match mood). *Aftenposten*, Oslo, Norway, 15 December, p. 34.

Humphrey, S. E., Nahrgang, J. D. and Morgenson, F. P. (2007). Integrating motivational, social, and contextual work design features: A meta-analytic summary and theoretical extension of the work design literature. *Journal of Applied Psychology*, 92(2), 1332–1356.

Hurley, R. F. (2006). The decision to trust. *Harvard Business Review*, 84(9), 55–62.

Hyde, K. L., Lerch, J., Norton, A., Forgeard, M., Winner, E. and Evans, A. C. (2009). Musical training shapes structural brain development. *Journal of Neuroscience*, 29(10), 3019–3025.

Jackson, S. A. and Csíkszentmihályi, M. (1999). *Flow in Sports: The Keys to Optimal Experiences and Performance*. Human Kinetics, Windsor, Ontario, Canada.

Jackson, S. A., Thomas, P., Marsh, H. W. and Smethurst, C. J. (2001). Relationships between flow, self-concept, psychological skills, and performance. *Journal of Applied Sport Psychology*, 13, 129–153.

James, W. (1963). *William James in Psychical Research*. Murphy, G. and Ballon, R. V. (eds). Viking Press, New York, USA.

Jensen, E. P. (2008). *Brain-based Learning: A New Paradigm of Teaching*. Corwin Press, Thousand Oaks, California, USA.

Johanson, U. (1999) The profitability of investments in work life-oriented rehabilitation: A measurement of perceptions. *Personnel Review*, 26(5), 395–415.

Kang, H. J., Voleti, B., Hajszan, T., Rajkowska, G., Stockmeier, C. A., Licznerski, P., Lepack, A., Majik, M. S., Jeong, L. S., Banasr, M., Son, H. and Duman, R. S. (2012). Decreased expression of synapse-related genes and loss of synapses in major depressive disorder. *Nature Medicine*, 18, 1413–1417.

Keynes, J. M. (2011). Quoted in the *Financial Times*, 27 December.

King, B. J. and Chapin, K. (1974). *Billie Jean*. Harper and Row, New York, USA.

Klein, D. B. (1984). *The Conception of Consciousness: A Survey*. University of Nebraska Press, Lincoln, Nebraska, USA.

Klein, S. (2005). *Lykkeformelen* (The happiness formula). Gyldendal Norsk Forlag, Oslo, Norway.

Kluger, J. (2013). The happiness of pursuit. *Time*, July 8–15, pp. 25–45.

Kohlberg, L. (1984). *Essays on Moral Development, Vol. II: The Psychology of Moral Development*. Harper and Row, San Francisco, USA.

Kohn, A. (1999). *Punished by Rewards: The Trouble with Gold Stars, Incentive Plans, A's, Praise, and other Bribes*. Houghton Mifflin, Boston, USA.

Korsvold, K. (2014). *Lærer musikk, blir flinkere* (Learns music, improves performance). *Aftenposten*, Oslo, Norway, 10 March, p. 8.

Kreidler, M. (1989). The zone. *The San Diego Union*, The Back Page, 18 June. San Diego, USA.

Kuhnert, K. W. and Lewis, P. (1987). Transactional and transformational leadership: A constructive/developmental analysis. *Academy of Management Review*, 12, 648–657.

Leonard, G. (1974). *The Ultimate Athlete: Re-visioning Sports, Physical Education, and the Body*. Avon Books, New York, USA.

Lindenberger, U., Li, S-C., Gruber, W. and Müller, V. (2009). Brains swinging in concert: Cortical phase synchronization while playing guitar. *BMC Neuroscience*, 10:22 (17 March).

Loevinger, J. (1976). *Ego Development: Conceptions and Theories*. Jossey-Bass, San Francisco, USA.

Loevinger J., Cohn, L. D., Bonneville, L. P., Redmore, C. D., Streich, D. D. and Sargent, M. (1985). Ego development in college. *Journal of Personality and Sociological Psychology*, 48, 947–962.

Long, T., Pantale′on, N., Bruant, G. and d'Arripe-Longueville, F. A. (2006). Qualitative study of moral reasoning of young elite athletes. *Sport Psychology*, 20, 330–347.

Luby, J. L., Barcha, D. M., Beldena, A., Gaffreya, M. S., Tillmana, R., Babba, C., Nishinoa, T., Suzukia, H. and Botteron, K. N. (2012). Maternal support in early childhood predicts larger hippocampal volumes at school age. *Proceedings of the National Academy of Sciences*, 109(8), 2854–2859.

Ludwig, M. (2011). *Brain Activation and Cortical Thickness in Experienced Meditators*. Dissertation. The California School of Professional Psychology, Alliant International University, San Diego, USA.

Lutz, A., Slagter, H., Dunne, J. D. and Davidson, R. J. (2008). Attention regulation and monitoring in meditation. *Trends in Cognitive Sciences*, 12, 163–169.

Lynch, D. (2014). uk.tm.org/creativity, as per 22 October.

Macnamara, B. N., Hambrick, D. Z. and Oswald, F. L. (2014). Deliberate practice and performance in music, games, sports, education, and professions: A meta-analysis. *Psychological Science*, 25(8), 1608–1618.

Madsen, P. A. (2013). *Jakten på spillets trone* (Chase for the game's throne). *Aftenposten*, Oslo, Norway, 16 November, kommentarer, p. 3.

Maguire, E. A, Woollett, K. and Spiers, H. J. (2006). London taxi drivers and bus drivers: A structural MRI and neuropsychological analysis. *Hippocampus*, 16(12), 1091–1101.

Maharishi Mahesh Yogi. ([1963] 2001). *Science of Being and Art of Living: Transcendental Meditation*. Revised and updated edition. Plume (a member of Penguin Putnam), New York, USA.

Maharishi Mahesh Yogi. (1969). *On the Bhagavad-Gita: A New Translation and Commentary*. Chapters 1–6. Penguin, Baltimore, Maryland, USA.

Maharishi Mahesh Yogi. (1976a). The scientific age is rising to be the Age of Enlightenment. Foreword in Orme-Johnson, D. W. and Farrow, J. (eds), *Scientific Research on the Transcendental Meditation Program: Collected Papers*, vol. 1, 1–4. Maharishi European Research University, Weggis, Switzerland.

Maharishi Mahesh Yogi. (1976b). *Creating an Ideal Society*. MERU Press Publication 1530, Rheinweiler, West Germany.

Maharishi Mahesh Yogi. (1986). *Life Supported by Natural Law*. Maharishi International University Press, Fairfield, Iowa, USA.

Maharishi Mahesh Yogi. (1995). *Maharishi's Absolute Theory of Government: Automation in Administration*. (2nd ed.). Age of Enlightenment Publications, India.

Maharishi Mahesh Yogi. (1997). *Celebrating Perfection in Education*. MUM Press, Fairfield, Iowa, USA.

Martin, W. and Ott, M. (2013). *The Cosmic View of Albert Einstein*. Sterling Publishing, New York, USA.

Maslow, A. H. (1968). *Toward a Psychology of Being* (2nd ed). Van Nostrand Reinhold, New York, USA.

Maslow, A. H. (1971). *The Farther Reaches of Human Nature*. The Viking Press, New York, USA.

Maslow, A. H. (1998). *Maslow on Management*. John Wiley & Sons, Inc., New York, USA.

Mason, L. I., Alexander, C. N., Travis, F. T., Marsh, G., Orme-Johnson, D. W., Gackenbach, J., Mason, D. C., Rainforth, M. and Walton, K. G. (1997). Electrophysiological correlates of higher states of consciousness during sleep in long-term practitioners of the Transcendental Meditation program. *Sleep*, 20(2), 102–110.

Mauboussin, M. J. (2009). *Think Twice: Harnessing the Power of Counterintuition*. Harvard Business School Press, Massachusetts, USA.

McCollum B. (1999). Leadership development and self development: An empirical study. *Career Development International*, 4(3), 149–154.

Merron, K., Fisher, D. and Torbert, W. R. (1987). Meaning making and management action. *Group and Organization Studies*, 12, 274–286.

Miller, A. (2014), dailyquoteboard.blogspot.com, 23 October.

Morgan, N. A. and Rego, L. L. (2009). Brand portfolio strategy and firm performance. *Journal of Marketing*, 73, 59–74.

Myklemyr, A. (2001). *Laget skal ta ansvar* (The team must assume responsibility). *Ukeavisen Ledelse*, Oslo, Norway, 23 November, pp. 17–18.

Myklemyr, A. (2008). *Sjefstreneren* (The boss coach). *Ukeavisen Ledelse*, Oslo, Norway, 25 January, pp. 24–26.

Natland, T. M. (2008). *Liten effekt av trenerbyttene* (Little effect of coach replacements). Master thesis, Høgskolen i Molde (Molde University College), Molde, Norway.

Newsweek. (2012). Green rankings 2012: U.S. companies, 22 October.

NOVA. (2013). *Norsk Institutt for forskning om oppvekst, velferd og aldring* (Norwegian institute for research on growing up, well-being, and aging). Reported in *Aftenposten*, Oslo, Norway, 10 October, pp. 8–9.

OECD. (2014). How was life? Global well-being since 1820, September.

Olsen, M. N. and Skodvin, H. (2013). Pengene eller livet (Money or life). *Morgenbladet*, Oslo, Norway, 25–31 October.

O'Neill, S. (1999). Flow theory and the development of musical performance skills. *Bulletin of the Council for Research in Music Education*, 141, 129–134.

Orme-Johnson, D. W., Alexander, C. N., Davies, J. L., Chandler, H. M. and Larimore, W. E. (1988). International peace project in the Middle East: The effect of the Maharishi Technology of the Unified Field. *Journal of Conflict Resolution*, 32, 776–812.

Orme-Johnson, D. W. and Walton, K. G. (1998). All approaches to preventing and reversing the effects of stress are not the same. *American Journal of Health Promotion*, 12(5), 297–299.

Panzarella, R. (1980). The phenomenology of aesthetic peak experiences. *Journal of Humanistic Psychology*, 20, 69–85.

Parnell, J. A. and Dent, E. B. (2009). The role of luck in the strategy-performance relationship. *Management Decision*, 47(6), 1000–1021.

Pearson, C. (2008). *The Complete Book of Yogic Flying: Maharishi Mahesh Yogi's Program for Enlightenment and Invincibility*. MUM Press, Fairfield, Iowa, USA.

Pearson, C. (2013). *The Supreme Awakening: Experiences of Enlightenment Throughout Time—And How You Can Cultivate Them*. MUM Press, Fairfield, Iowa, USA.

Pelé and Fish, R. L. (1977). *My Life and the Beautiful Game: The Autobiography of Pelé*. Doubleday, Garden City, New York, USA.

Pensgaard, A. M. and Roberts, G. C. (2000). The relationship between motivational climate, perception of ability and sources of stress among elite athletes. *Journal of Sport Science*, 18, 191–200.

Petsche, H. (1996). Approaches to verbal, visual and musical creativity by EEG coherence analysis. *International Journal of Psychophysiology*, 24(1–2), 145–159.

Pfeffer, J. and Sutton, R. I. (2006). *Hard Facts, Dangerous Half-Truths, and Total Nonsense: Profiting from Evidence-Based Management*. Harvard Business School Publishing, Boston, Massachusetts, USA.

Pfurtscheller G., Neuper C., Flotzinger D. and Pregenzer, M. (1997). EEG-based discrimination between imagination of right and left hand movement, *Electroencephalography and Clinical Neurophysiology*, 103(6), 642–651.

Piaget, J. (1954). *The Construction of Reality in the Child*. Basic Books, New York, USA.

Piaget, J. (1972). Intellectual evolution from adolescence to adulthood. *Human Development*, 15, 1–12.

Picasso, P. (2014). http://burgher-art-facts.tripod.com/index.html, 18 October.

Poloma, M. M. and Pendleton, B. F. (1991). *Exploring Neglected Dimensions of Religion in Quality of Life Research*. Edwin Mellon Press, Lewiston, New York, USA.

Privette, G. (1983). Peak experiences, peak performance, and flow: A comparative analysis of positive human experiences. *Journal of Personality and Social Psychology*, 45, 1361–1368.

Raichele, M. E. (2010). The brain's dark energy. *Scientific American*, March, 44–49.

Ravizza, K. (1977). Peak experiences in sports. *Journal of Humanistic Psychology*, 17(4), 35–40.

Reddy, M. K., Bai, A. J. L. and Rao, V. R. (1977). The effects of the Transcendental Meditation program on athletic performance. In Orme-Johnson, D. W. and Farrow, J. T. (eds), *Scientific Research on the Transcendental Meditation Program, Collected Papers*. Maharishi University of Management, Fairfield, Iowa, USA, 1, 346–358.

Reingold, J. and Underwood, R. (2004). *Fast Company*. Gruner & Jahr USA Publishing, New York, USA.

Rich, B. L., Lepine, J. A. and Crawford, E. R. (2010). Job engagement: Antecedents and effects on job performance. *Academy of Management Journal*, 53, 617–635.

Robertson, I. T. and Smith, J. M. (2001). Personnel selection. *Journal of Occupational and Organizational Psychology*, 74, 441–472.

Roderick, G. and Kilts, C. (2007). Cognitive fitness. *Harvard Business Review*, 85(11), 53–66.

Rooke, D. and Torbert, W. R. (2005). Seven transformations of leadership. *Harvard Business Review*, April.

Rosenthal, N. (2011). *Transcendence: Healing and Transformation through Transcendental Meditation*. Jeremy P. Tarcher/Penguin, New York, USA.

Russell, W. F. and Branch, T. (1979). *Second Wind: The Memoirs of an Opinionated Man*. Random House, New York, USA.

Sacks, J. D. (2015). *Verdens fattigdom synker* (Declining poverty in the world). *Aftenposten*, Oslo, Norway, 8 January, p. 10.

Salvador, R. and Folger, R. G. (2009). Business ethics and the brain. *Business Ethics Quarterly*, 19(1), 1–31.

Schmidt, F. L. and Hunter, J. E. (1998). The validity and utility of selection methods in personnel psychology: Practical and theoretical implications of 85 years of research findings. *Psychology Bulletin*, 124(2), 262–274.

Schmidt-Wilk J. (2000). Consciousness-based management development: Case studies of international top management teams. *Journal of Transnational Management Development*, 5(3), 61–85.

Schmidt-Wilk J. (2003). TQM and the Transcendental Meditation program in a Swedish top management team. *The TQM Magazine*, 15(4), 219–229.

Schmuck, P. et al. (2000). Intrinsic and extrinsic goals: Their structure and relationship to well-being in German and US college students. *Social Indicators Research*, 50, 225–241.

Schneider, R. H., Alexander, C. N., Staggers, F., Orme-Johnson, D. W., Rainforth, M., Salerno, J. W., Sheppard, W., Castillo-Richmond, A., Barnes, V. A. and Nidich, S. I. (2005). A randomized controlled trial of stress reduction in the treatment of hypertension in African Americans during one year. *American Journal of Hypertension*, 18(1), 88–98.

Schneider, R. H., Grim, C. E., Rainforth, M. V., Kotchen, T., Nidich, S. I., Gaylord-King, C., Salerno, J. W., Kotchen, J. M. and Alexander, C. N. (2012). Stress reduction in the secondary prevention of cardiovascular disease: Randomized, controlled trial of Transcendental Meditation and health education in blacks. *Circulation: Cardiovascular Quality and Outcomes*, 5, 750–758.

Sedlmeier, P., Eberth, J., Schwarz, M., Zimmermann, D., Haarig, F. and Jaeger, S. (2012). The psychological effects of meditation: A meta-analysis. *Psychology Bulletin*, 138(6), 1139–1171.

Segal, M. (2004). History of neuroscience: Dendritic spines and memory. IBRO History of Neuroscience, International Brain Research Organization—ibro.org.

Seinfeld, J. (2014). www.changebeginswithin.org/advisors.html, 22 October.

Senge, P. M. (1994). *The Fifth Discipline: The Art and Practice of the Learning Organization* (1st ed.). Doubleday, New York, USA.

Shields D. L. and Bredemeier, B. J. (2001). Moral development and behavior in sport. In Singer, R. N., Hausenblas, H. A. and Janelle, C. M. (eds), *Handbook of Sport Psychology*. Wiley, New York, USA, 585–603.

Skorstad, E. (2008). *Rett person på rett plass* (Right person in the right place). Gyldendal Akademisk forlag, Oslo, Norway.

Smith, P. A. C. and Peters, J. (1996). The corporate leadership crisis: Break out this way. *The Learning Organization: An International Journal*, 4(2), 61–69.

Smith, J. M. and Smith, P. (2005). *Testing People at Work: Competencies in Psychometric Testing*. Blackwell, Malden, Middlesex County, Massachusetts, USA.

Stellar, J. E., John-Henderson, N., Anderson, C. L., Gordon, A. M., McNeil, G. D. and Keltner, D. (2015). Positive affect and markers of inflammation: Discrete positive emotions predict lower levels of inflammatory cytokines. *Emotion*, DOI: 10.1037/emo0000033.

Steptoe, A. and Wardle, J. (2011). Positive affect measured using ecological momentary assessment and survival in older men and women. *Proceedings of the National Academy of Sciences*, USA, 31 October.

Storm, J. F. (2014). *På sporet av bevisstheten* (On the track of consciousness). *Aftenposten*, Oslo, Norway, 6 April, pp. 12–13.

Stroop, J. (1935). Studies of interference in serial verbal reactions. *Journal of Experimental Psychology*, 18, 643–662.

Subramaniam, K., Kounios, J., Barrish, T. B. and Jung-Beeman, M. (2009). A brain mechanism for facilitating insight by positive affect. *Journal of Cognitive Neuroscience*, 21(3), 415–432.

Taylor, A. III. (1997). How Toyota defies gravity. *Fortune*, 8 December.

The Performance Group. (1993). *A Study of World-class Performers: The Gateway to High Performance*. Oslo, Norway.

Toga, A. W., Thompson, P. M. and Sowell, E. R. (2006). Mapping brain maturation. *Trends in Neurosciences*, 29(3), 148–159.

Torbert, W. R. (1991). *The Power of Balance: Transforming Self, Society, and Scientific Inquiry*. Sage Publications, Newbury Park, California, USA.

Travis, F. and Pearson, C. (2000). Pure consciousness: Distinct phenomenological and physiological correlates of "consciousness itself." *The International Journal of Neuroscience*, 100, 1–10.

Travis, F., Tecce, J., Arenander, A. and Wallace, R. K. (2002). Patterns of EEG coherence, power, and contingent negative variation characterize the integration of transcendental and waking states. *Biological Psychology*, 61, 293–319.

Travis, F., Arenander, A. and DuBois, D. (2004). Psychological and physiological characteristics of a proposed object-referral/self-referral continuum of self-awareness. *Consciousness and Cognition*, 13(2), 401–420.

Travis, F. and Brown, S. (2009). My brain made me do it: Brain maturation and levels of self-development. In Pfaffenberger, A. H., Marko, P. W. and

Greening, T. (eds), *The Postconventional Personality: Perspectives on Higher Development*. Sage Publishing, New York, USA.

Travis, F., Haaga, D. H., Hagelin, J., Tanner, M., Nidich, S., Gaylord-King, C., Grosswald, S., Rainforth, M. and Schneider, R. (2009). Effects of Transcendental Meditation practice on brain functioning and stress reactivity in college students. *International Journal of Psychophysiology*, 71, 170–176.

Travis, F. and Shear, J. (2010). Focused attention, open monitoring and automatic self-transcending: Categories to organize meditations from Vedic, Buddhist and Chinese traditions. *Consciousness and Cognition*, 19, 1110–1119.

Travis, F., Haaga, D.H., Hagelin, J., Tanner, M., A., Nidich, S., Gaylord-King, C., Grosswald, S., Rainforth, M. and Schneider, R. (2010). A self-referral default brain state: Patterns of coherence, power, and eLORETA sources during eyes-closed rest and the Transcendental Meditation practice. *Cognitive Processing*, 11(1), 21–30.

Travis, F., Harung, H. S. and Lagrosen, Y. (2011). Moral development, executive functioning, peak experiences and brain patterns in professional and amateur classical musicians: Interpreted in light of a unified theory of performance. *Consciousness and Cognition*, 20(4), 1256–1264.

Travis, F. (2012a). *Your Brain is a River, not a Rock*. Fairfield, Iowa, USA: ftravis@mum.edu.

Travis, F. (2012b). Core and matrix thalamic nuclei: Parallel circuits involved in content of experience and general wakefulness. *NeuroQuantology*, 10(2), 144–149.

Travis, F. and Lagrosen, Y. (2014). Creativity and brain-functioning in product development engineers: A canonical correlation analysis. *Creativity Research Journal*, 26(2), 239–243.

Trevino, L. K. and Nelson, K. A. (2007). *Managing Business Ethics*. Wiley, New York, USA.

Tutko, T. and Tosi, U. (1976). *Sports Psyching: Playing your Best Game All of the Time*. J. P. Tarcher, Los Angeles, California, USA.

Vestberg, T., Gustafson, R., Maurex, L., Ingvar, M. and Petrovic, P. (2012). Executive functions predict the success of top-soccer players. *PLoS One*, 7(4), e34731. doi: 10.1371/journal.pone.0034731.

Waldman, D. A., Balthazard, P. A. and Peterson, S. (2011). The neuroscience of leadership: Can we revolutionize the way that leaders are identified and developed? *Academy of Management Perspectives*, 25(1), 60–74.

Wheatley, M. J. (1994). *Leadership and the New Science: Learning about Organization from an Orderly Universe*. Berrett-Koehler, San Francisco, California, USA.

Wigner, E. (1970). *Symmetries and Reflections: Scientific Essays*. M.I.T. Press, Cambridge, Massachusetts, USA.

Wilber, K. (2000). *Integral Psychology: Consciousness, Spirit, Psychology, Therapy*. Shambhala, Boston, USA.

World Plan Films. (1976). The Transcendental Meditation program in baseball. Institute for Fitness and Athletic Excellence, USA. An edited version of the video is on YouTube: Transcendental Meditation in Baseball.

Wulff, D. M. (1991). *Psychology of Religion: Classic and Contemporary Views*. John Wiley, New York, USA.

Wuthnow, R. (1978). Peak experiences: Some empirical tests. *Journal of Humanistic Psychology*, 18(3), 59–75.

Yau, S. T. and Nadis, S. (2010). *The Shape of Inner Space: String Theory and the Geometry of the Universe's Hidden Dimensions*. Amazon.com.

Yang, M. (2012). Confusion-based theory of management: A qualitative study of Chinese mid-level managers. Ph.D. Dissertation, Maharishi University of Management, Fairfield, Iowa, USA.

Zes, D. and Landis, D. (2013). A better return on self-awareness. Companies with higher rates of return on stock also have employees with fewer personal blind spots. Korn/Ferry Institute, August.

Zuk, J., Benjamin, C., Kenyon, A. and Gaab, N. (2014). Behavioral and neural correlates of executive functioning in musicians and non-musicians. *PLoS ONE*, 9(6), e99868. doi:10.1371/journal.pone.0099868.

Index

(Figures indexed with bold page numbering. For a list of tables see p. xi)